D1356261

# RAIL ATLAS
# GREAT BRITAIN
# & IRELAND

Compiled by **S.K. Baker**

## Oxford Publishing Co.

Seventh Edition
© 1992 S. K. Baker & Haynes Publishing Group

A catalogue record for this book is available from the
British Library.

ISBN 0 86093 502 7

Library of Congress catalog card number
91-76785

The publisher asks that readers should note that the background map of the cover
has been taken from the previous 6th Edition and is therefore not fully up to date.

Oxford Publishing Co. is part of the
Haynes Publishing Group PLC
Sparkford, Near Yeovil, Somerset, BA22 7JJ

Haynes Publications Inc.
861 Lawrence Drive, Newbury Park, California 91320 USA

Printed by: J. H. Haynes & Co. Ltd.
Typeset in Univers Roman Medium

Front cover illustrations:

Top left: Class 47 No. 47853 passes Pokesdown on 29th
August 1991 with the 10.40 Poole-Glasgow 'Wessex Scot'.
(Brian Denton)

Top right: Class 60 No. 60033 Anthony Ashley Cooper is near
Worgret Junction on 28th June 1991 with 6V29, the 19.44
Furzebrook-Hallen Marsh LPG working. (Brian Denton)

Below left: 2-6-2T No. 8 in Cambrian Railways black livery
awaits departure from Aberystwyth on the 1ft 11½ in gauge
Vale of Rheidol Railway with the 11.00 train to Devil's Bridge,
21st April 1990. (Peter Nicholson)

Below right: Refurbished 'Centro' liveried Class 150/1 'Sprinter'
crosses Penrhyndeudraeth bridge, forming the 09.38 Pwllheli-
Machynlleth train on 20th August 1991. (Stuart Baker).

## GLOSSARY OF ABBREVIATIONS

| | | | |
|---|---|---|---|
| ABM | Associated British Maltsters | IE | Iarnrod Eireann (Irish Rail) |
| ABP | Associated British Ports | LIFT | London International Freight Terminal |
| ARC | Amey Roadstone Company | L.L. | Low Level |
| ASW | Allied Steel & Wire | LUL | London Underground Limited |
| B & I | British & Irish Line | MDHC | Mersey Docks & Harbour Company |
| BC | British Coal | M&EE | Mechanical and Electrical Engineer |
| BIS | British Industrial Sand | MoD | Ministry of Defence |
| BOC | British Oxygen Company | MSC | Manchester Ship Canal |
| BP | British Petroleum | NFD | National Fuel Distributors |
| BR | British Rail | NIR | Northern Ireland Railways |
| BWB | British Waterways Board | OLE | Overhead Line Equipment |
| C. & W. | Carriage and Wagon | PO | Post Office |
| Cal-Mac | Caledonian MacBrayne | P.S. | Power Station |
| C.C. | County Council | PTE | Passenger Transport Executive |
| CE | Civil Engineer | P.W. | Permanent Way |
| C.S. | Carriage Sidings | RMC | Ready Mix Concrete (Marcon) |
| DCL | Distillers Company Limited | RPSI | Railway Preservation Society of Ireland |
| Dist | Distribution | S. & T. | Signal & Telegraph |
| D.P. | Disposal Point | SAI | Scottish Agricultural Industries |
| ECC | English China Clays | SGD | Scottish Grain Distillers |
| EMU | Electric Multiple Unit | SMD | Scottish Malt Distillers |
| FLT | Freightliner Terminal | Term. | Terminal |
| GEC | General Electric Company | UES | United Engineering Steels |
| H.L. | High Level | UKAEA | United Kingdom Atomic Energy Authority |
| ICI | Imperial Chemical Industries | | |

# PREFACE TO FIRST EDITION

The inspiration for this atlas was two-fold; firstly a feeling of total bewilderment by 'Llans' and 'Abers' on first visiting South Wales four years ago, and secondly a wall railway map drawn by a friend, Martin Bairstow. Since then, at university, there has been steady progress in drawing the rail network throughout Great Britain. The author feels sure that this atlas as it has finally evolved will be useful to all with an interest in railways, whether professional or enthusiast. The emphasis is on the current network since it is felt that this information is not published elsewhere.

Throughout, the main aim has been to show clearly, using expanded sheets where necessary, the railways of this country, including the whole of London Transport and light railways. Passenger lines are distinguished by colour according to operating company and all freight-only lines are depicted in red. The criterion for a British Rail passenger line has been taken as at least one advertised passenger train per day in each direction. On passenger routes, to assist the traveller, single and multiple track sections, with crossing loops on single lines have been shown. Symbols are used to identify both major centres of rail freight, such as collieries and power stations, and railway installations such as locomotive depots and works. Secondary information, for example junction names and tunnels over 100 yards long, with lengths if over one mile has been shown.

The author would like to express his thanks to members of the Oxford University Railway Society and to Nigel Bird, Chris Hammond and Richard Warson in particular for help in compiling and correcting the maps. His cousin, Dr Tony McCann deserves special thanks for removing much of the tedium by computer sorting the index, as do Oxford City Libraries for providing excellent reference facilities.

June 1977

# PREFACE TO SEVENTH EDITION

This seventh edition of the *Rail Atlas of Great Britain and Ireland* has been fully updated to show the many changes in the rail network over recent years. Six additional insets have been added to expand the presentation of the Exeter, Reading, Ipswich, Shrewsbury, Bletchley and Limerick Junction areas.

The numerous changes include proposals for some significant new railways, many new passenger stations but a net decline in freight terminals – particularly smaller locations and collieries. Many towns and cities are developing Light Rapid Transit proposals: the new Manchester Metrolink, the Sheffield Supertram (under construction) and the other current schemes are shown.

The author would like to thank the many people who have contacted him to supply material for this new edition. Thanks are also due to his family for their patience and support.

Stuart K. Baker
York
March 1992

# CONTENTS

### Publisher's Note

Although situations are constantly changing on the railways of Britain every effort has been made by the author to ensure complete accuracy of the maps in the book at the time of going to press.

# KEY TO ATLAS

| | | Surface | Tunnel | Tube |
|---|---|---|---|---|
| British Rail – Passenger<br>Also Irish and Isle of Man Railways | Multiple Track | —————— | ]- -[ | - - - - - |
| | Single Track | +++++++++++++ | +++]- -[+++ | - - - - - |
| Municipal & Urban Railways<br>*(London Underground Ltd<br>lines indicated by code)* | Multiple Track | C<br>—————— | C<br>]- -[ | C<br>- - - - |
| | Single Track | C<br>+++++++++++ | C<br>+++]- -[+++ | C<br>- - - - |
| Preserved & Minor Passenger Railways<br>*(With name, and gauge where<br>other than standard gauge)* | Multiple Track | —————— | ]- -[ | |
| | Single Track | +++++++++++++ | +++]- -[+++ | |
| Freight only lines —<br>*(British Rail & Others)* | No Single/<br>Multiple<br>Distinction | —————— | ]- -[ | |

Advertised Passenger Station :  Saltburn ●

Crossing Loop at Passenger Station :  Newtown +++++✕+++++

Crossing Loop on Single Line :  Kincraig +++++✕+++++

Unadvertised/Excursion Station :  Ennis * ●

| | | | |
|---|---|---|---|
| Major Power Signal boxes | <u>PRESTON</u> | Line Ownership Boundaries | BR ¦ LUL |
| Carriage Sidings | ——— C.S. | Colliery (incl. Washery & Opencast site) | ▲ |
| Freight Marshalling Yard | ▱ | Power Station | △ |
| Freightliner Terminal | ——— FLT | Oil Refinery | ● |
| Locomotive Depot/Stabling Point | ■ BS | Oil Terminal | ○ |
| British Rail Engineering Ltd. | ▨ BREL | Cement Works or Terminal | ■ |
| British Rail Maintenance Ltd. | ▨ BRML | Quarry | □ |
| Junction Names | *Haughley Junc.* | Other Freight Terminal | ┤ |
| Country Border | ///////// | County Boundary | - - - - |

# DIAGRAM OF MAPS

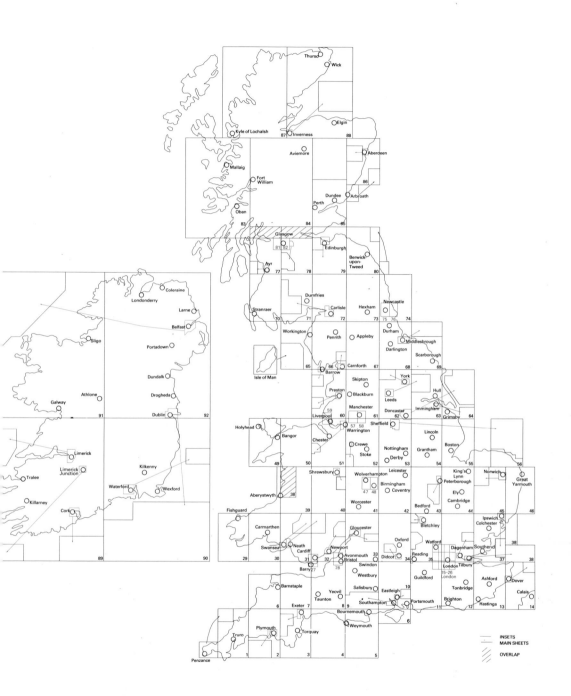

INSETS
MAIN SHEETS
OVERLAP

v

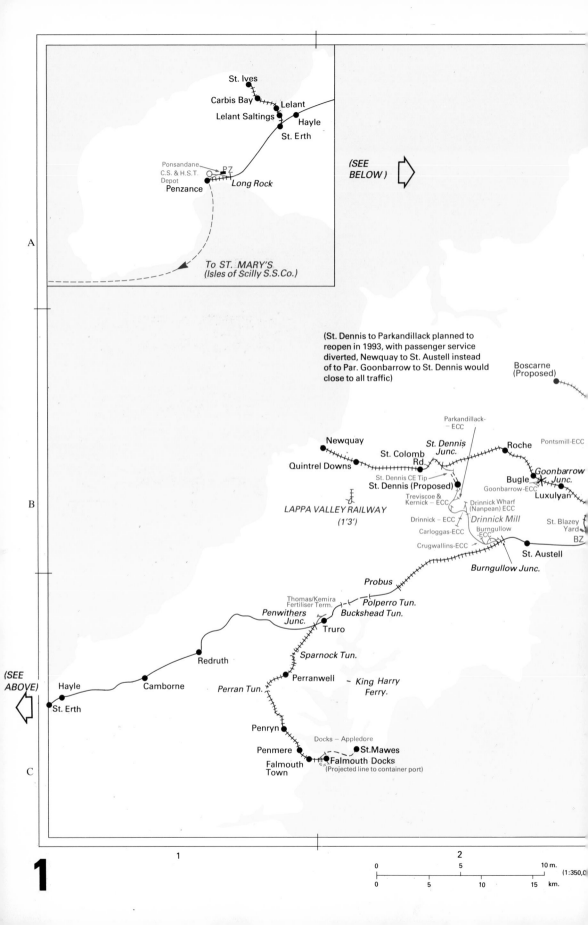

**(SEE BELOW)** →

St. Ives
Carbis Bay
Lelant
Lelant Saltings
Hayle
St. Erth

Ponsandane
C.S. & H.S.T.
Depot
P7
Long Rock
Penzance

To ST. MARY'S
(Isles of Scilly S.S.Co.)

A

(St. Dennis to Parkandillack planned to reopen in 1993, with passenger service diverted, Newquay to St. Austell instead of to Par. Goonbarrow to St. Dennis would close to all traffic)

Boscarne
(Proposed)

Parkandillack
– ECC

Pontsmill-ECC

Newquay
St. Colomb
Rd.
St. Dennis
Junc.
Roche

Quintrel Downs
St. Dennis CE Tip
St. Dennis (Proposed)
Bugle
Goonbarrow
Junc.
Goonbarrow-ECC
Luxulyan

LAPPA VALLEY RAILWAY
(1'3')

Treviscoe &
Kernick – ECC
Drinnick Wharf
(Nanpean) ECC

St. Blazey
Yard

Drinnick – ECC
Drinnick Mill

BZ

Carloggas-ECC
Burngullow
-ECC

Crugwallins-ECC

St. Austell

B

Burngullow Junc.

Probus

Thomas/Kemira
Fertiliser Term.
Polperro Tun.
Penwithers
Junc.
Buckshead Tun.
Truro

Sparnock Tun.

Redruth
Perranwell
King Harry
Ferry.

Hayle
Camborne
Perran Tun.

**(SEE ABOVE)** ←

St. Erth

Penryn

Docks – Appledore

Penmere
St.Mawes
Falmouth Docks
Falmouth
Town
(Projected line to container port)

C

1
2

0    5    10 m.
(1:350,0
0    5    10    15  km.

**1**

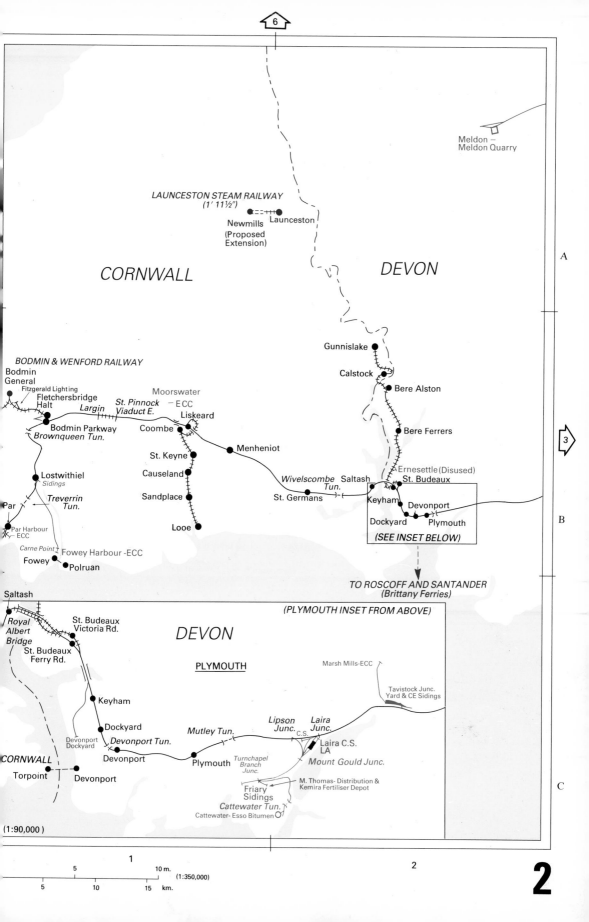

Meldon –
Meldon Quarry

LAUNCESTON STEAM RAILWAY
(1' 11½")

Newmills          Launceston
(Proposed
Extension)

CORNWALL                    DEVON

Gunnislake

Calstock

Bere Alston

BODMIN & WENFORD RAILWAY
Bodmin
General
Fitzgerald Lighting
Fletchersbridge        Moorswater
Halt                   — ECC
Largin    St. Pinnock
          Viaduct E.        Liskeard
Bodmin Parkway   Coombe
Brownqueen Tun.

Bere Ferrers

St. Keyne        Menheniot

Lostwithiel        Causeland
Sidings
                Sandplace        Wivelscombe    Saltash    Ernesettle (Disused)
Par      Treverrin                Tun.                      St. Budeaux
         Tun.                   St. Germans        Keyham
Par Harbour                      Looe                      Devonport
— ECC                                         Dockyard    Plymouth
Carne Point   Fowey Harbour -ECC
Fowey    Polruan                                   (SEE INSET BELOW)

A

3

B

TO ROSCOFF AND SANTANDER
(Brittany Ferries)

Saltash                      (PLYMOUTH INSET FROM ABOVE)

Royal            St. Budeaux       DEVON
Albert           Victoria Rd.
Bridge                                           Marsh Mills-ECC
     St. Budeaux                PLYMOUTH
     Ferry Rd.
                                                     Tavistock Junc.
          Keyham                                     Yard & CE Sidings

          Dockyard       Mutley Tun.   Lipson    Laira
     Devonport                          Junc.    Junc.
     Dockyard   Devonport Tun.                 C.S.  Laira C.S.
CORNWALL    Devonport    Plymouth   Turnchapel        LA
                                    Branch        Mount Gould Junc.
Torpoint    Devonport              Junc.
                                         M. Thomas- Distribution &
                                    Friary   Kemira Fertiliser Depot
                                    Sidings
                                 Cattewater Tun.
                            Cattewater- Esso Bitumen

C

(1:90,000)

1                              2

5                    10 m.
                    (1:350,000)
5        10        15   km.

2

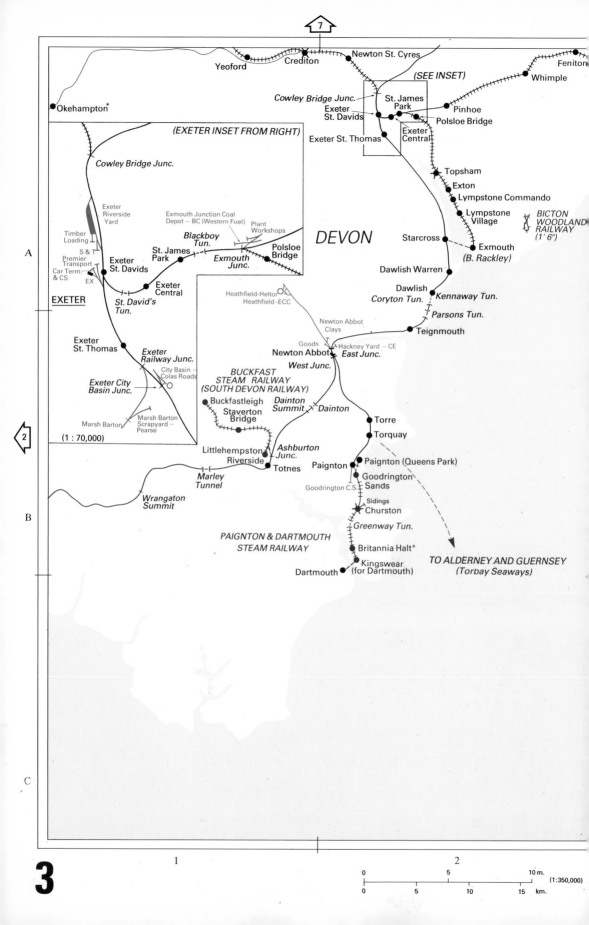

Yeoford
Crediton
Newton St. Cyres
Feniton
Whimple

*Cowley Bridge Junc.*
St. James Park
Exeter St. Davids
Pinhoe
Polsloe Bridge

Okehampton*

*(SEE INSET)*

Exeter St. Thomas
Exeter Central

*(EXETER INSET FROM RIGHT)*

*Cowley Bridge Junc.*

Topsham
Exton
Lympstone Commando
Lympstone Village

Exeter Riverside Yard

Exmouth Junction Coal Depot – BC (Western Fuel)

Plant Workshops

**DEVON**

Starcross
Exmouth (B. Rackley)

*BICTON WOODLAND RAILWAY (1' 6")*

Timber Loading
S & T
Premier Transport
Car Term. & CS
EX

*Blackboy Tun.*
St. James Park
*Exmouth Junc.*
Polsloe Bridge

Dawlish Warren

A

Exeter St. Davids
Exeter Central

Dawlish
*Coryton Tun.*
*Kennaway Tun.*

**EXETER**
*St. David's Tun.*

Heathfield-Heltor
Heathfield -ECC

*Parsons Tun.*

Newton Abbot Clays

Teignmouth

Exeter St. Thomas
*Exeter Railway Junc.*

Goods
Newton Abbot
Hackney Yard – CE
*West Junc.* *East Junc.*

City Basin – Colas Roads

*Exeter City Basin Junc.*

*BUCKFAST STEAM RAILWAY (SOUTH DEVON RAILWAY)*

Buckfastleigh
Staverton Bridge

*Dainton Summit*
*Dainton*

Torre
Torquay

Marsh Barton
Marsh Barton Scrapyard – Pearse

(1 : 70,000)

Littlehempstead
Riverside
*Ashburton Junc.*
Totnes

Paignton
Paignton (Queens Park)

Goodrington C.S.
Goodrington Sands

*Marley Tunnel*

B

*Wrangaton Summit*

Sidings
Churston

*TO ALDERNEY AND GUERNSEY (Torbay Seaways)*

*PAIGNTON & DARTMOUTH STEAM RAILWAY*

*Greenway Tun.*

Britannia Halt*

Dartmouth
Kingswear (for Dartmouth)

2

C

1
2

0          5          10 m.
(1:350,000)
0     5     10     15 km.

**3**

DEVON

Axminster

DORSET

Maiden Newton

SEATON TRAMWAY
Colyton
Cownhayne
Cownhayne
Tye Lane
Swans Nest
Colyford
Axmouth
Riverside
Seaton
Depot

8

A

5

B

C

1

2

5

10 m.

(1:350,000)

5          10          15      km.

4

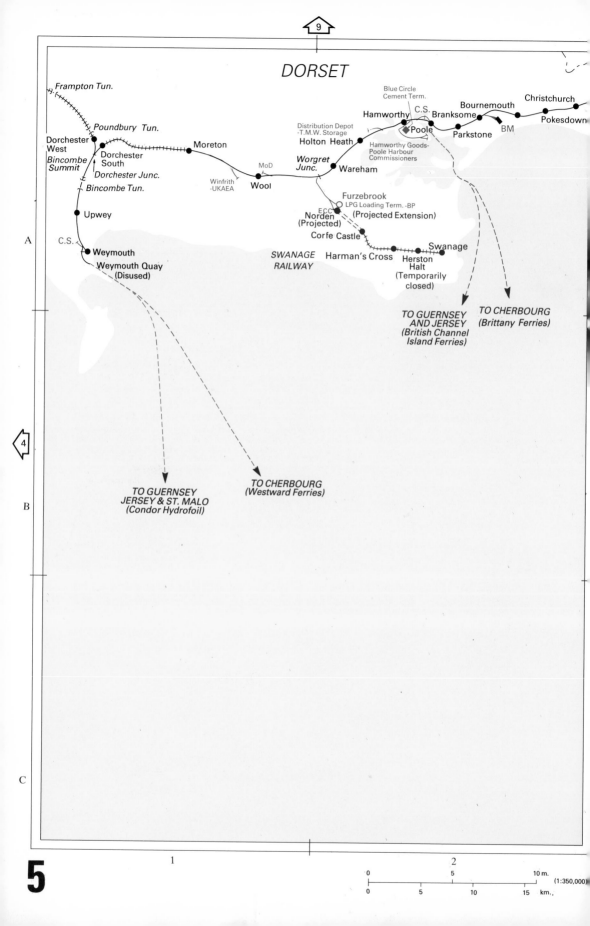

DORSET

Frampton Tun.

Poundbury Tun.

Dorchester
West

Bincombe
Summit

Dorchester
South

Dorchester Junc.

Bincombe Tun.

Moreton

Winfrith
-UKAEA

Wool

MoD

Distribution Depot
-T.M.W. Storage
Holton Heath

Worgret
Junc.

Wareham

Blue Circle
Cement Term.

Hamworthy

C.S.

Poole

Hamworthy Goods-
Poole Harbour
Commissioners

Branksome

Parkstone

Bournemouth

BM

Christchurch

Pokesdown

Upwey

C.S.

Weymouth

Weymouth Quay
(Disused)

Furzebrook
LPG Loading Term. -BP
(Projected Extension)

ECC
Norden
(Projected)

Corfe Castle

SWANAGE
RAILWAY

Harman's Cross

Herston
Halt
(Temporarily
closed)

Swanage

TO GUERNSEY
AND JERSEY
(British Channel
Island Ferries)

TO CHERBOURG
(Brittany Ferries)

TO GUERNSEY
JERSEY & ST. MALO
(Condor Hydrofoil)

TO CHERBOURG
(Westward Ferries)

A

4

B

C

1

2

0   5   10 m.
(1:350,000)
0   5   10   15 km.,

**5**

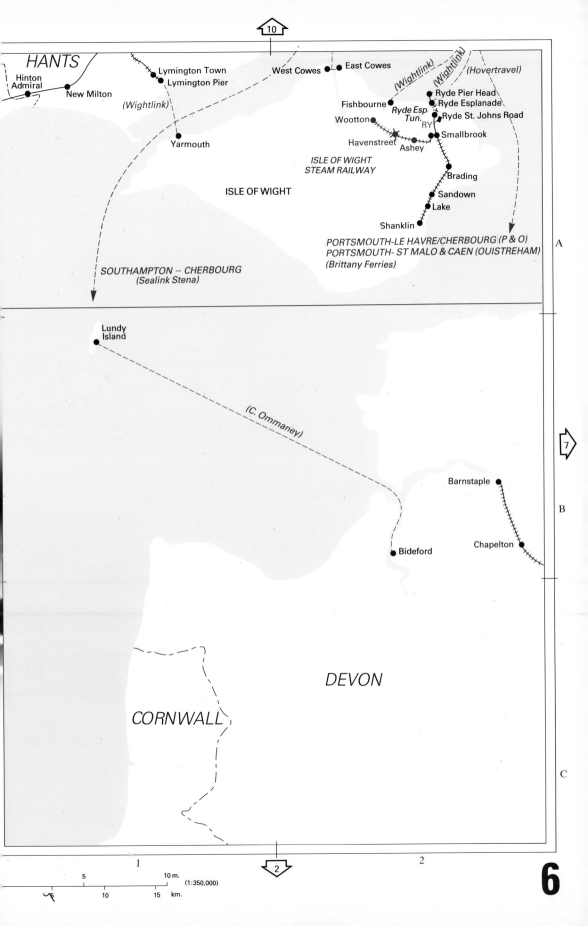

HANTS

Hinton Admiral

New Milton

Lymington Town
Lymington Pier

*(Wightlink)*

Yarmouth

West Cowes ● ● East Cowes

*(Wightlink)* *(Wightlink)* *(Hovertravel)*

Fishbourne

Wootton

*Ryde Esp. Tun.*
RY

Ryde Pier Head
Ryde Esplanade
Ryde St. Johns Road

Smallbrook

Havenstreet   Ashey

ISLE OF WIGHT STEAM RAILWAY

Brading

ISLE OF WIGHT

Sandown
Lake

Shanklin

*PORTSMOUTH-LE HAVRE/CHERBOURG (P & O)*
*PORTSMOUTH- ST MALO & CAEN (OUISTREHAM)*
*(Brittany Ferries)*

A

*SOUTHAMPTON – CHERBOURG*
*(Sealink Stena)*

Lundy Island

*(C. Ommaney)*

⬆ 7

Barnstaple

B

Chapelton

Bideford

DEVON

CORNWALL

C

1

5        10 m.

(1:350,000)

10       15   km.

2

⬇ 2

2

**6**

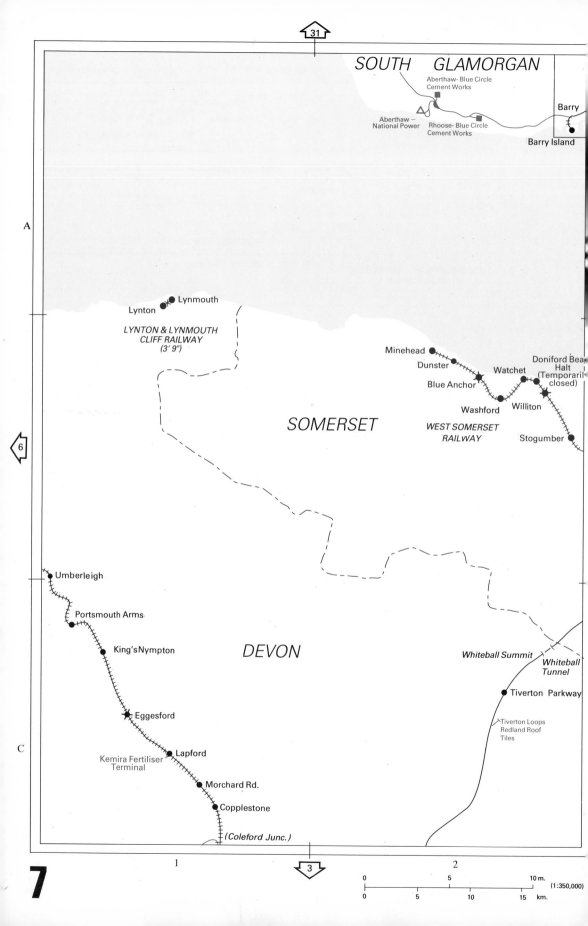

SOUTH GLAMORGAN

Aberthaw- Blue Circle
Cement Works

Aberthaw –
National Power

Rhoose- Blue Circle
Cement Works

Barry

Barry Island

A

Lynmouth
Lynton
LYNTON & LYNMOUTH
CLIFF RAILWAY
(3′ 9″)

Minehead
Dunster
Blue Anchor
Watchet
Doniford Bea
Halt
(Temporaril
closed)

SOMERSET

Washford
Williton

WEST SOMERSET
RAILWAY

6

Stogumber

Umberleigh

Portsmouth Arms

King's Nympton

DEVON

Whiteball Summit
Whiteball
Tunnel

Tiverton  Parkway

Eggesford

Tiverton Loops
Redland Roof
Tiles

C

Kemira Fertiliser
Terminal

Lapford

Morchard Rd.

Copplestone

(Coleford Junc.)

**7**

1

2

| 0 | | 5 | | 10 m. |
|---|---|---|---|---|

(1:350,000)

| 0 | | 5 | | 10 | | 15 | km. |
|---|---|---|---|---|---|---|---|

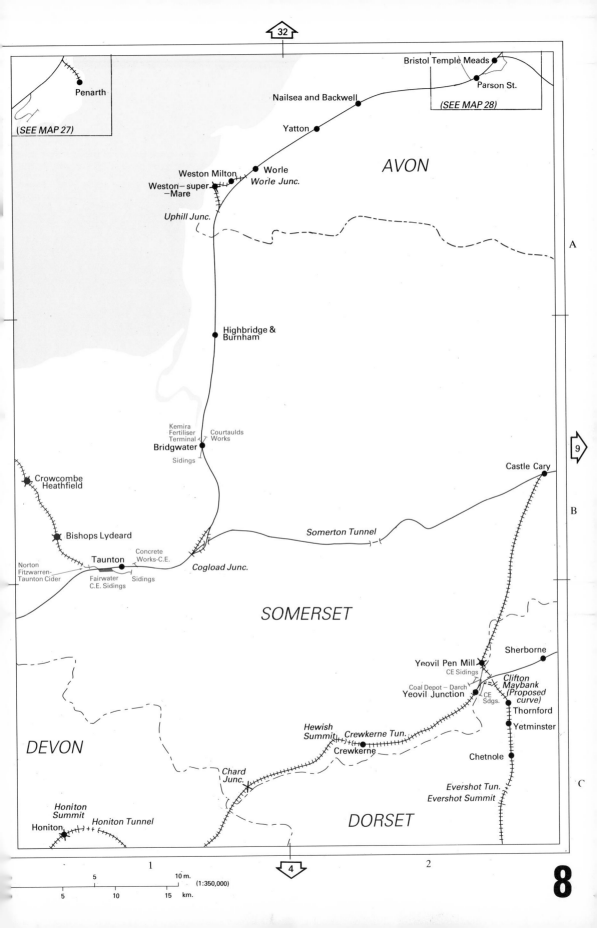

Penarth

(SEE MAP 27)

Bristol Temple Meads
Parson St.

Nailsea and Backwell

Yatton

(SEE MAP 28)

AVON

Weston Milton
Weston–super–Mare
Worle
Worle Junc.

Uphill Junc.

A

Highbridge & Burnham

9

Kemira Fertiliser Terminal
Courtaulds Works
Bridgwater
Sidings

Castle Cary

Crowcombe Heathfield

B

Somerton Tunnel

Bishops Lydeard

Concrete Works-C.E.

Taunton

Norton Fitzwarren-Taunton Cider
Fairwater C.E. Sidings
Sidings
Cogload Junc.

SOMERSET

Sherborne

Yeovil Pen Mill
CE Sidings

Clifton Maybank (Proposed curve)

Coal Depot – Darch
Yeovil Junction
CE Sdgs.

Thornford

Yetminster

Hewish Summit
Crewkerne Tun.

DEVON

Chard Junc.
Crewkerne

Chetnole

Eﬀershot Tun.
Evershot Summit

C

Honiton Summit
Honiton
Honiton Tunnel

DORSET

1
10 m.
5
(1:350,000)
5        10        15   km.
2

**8**

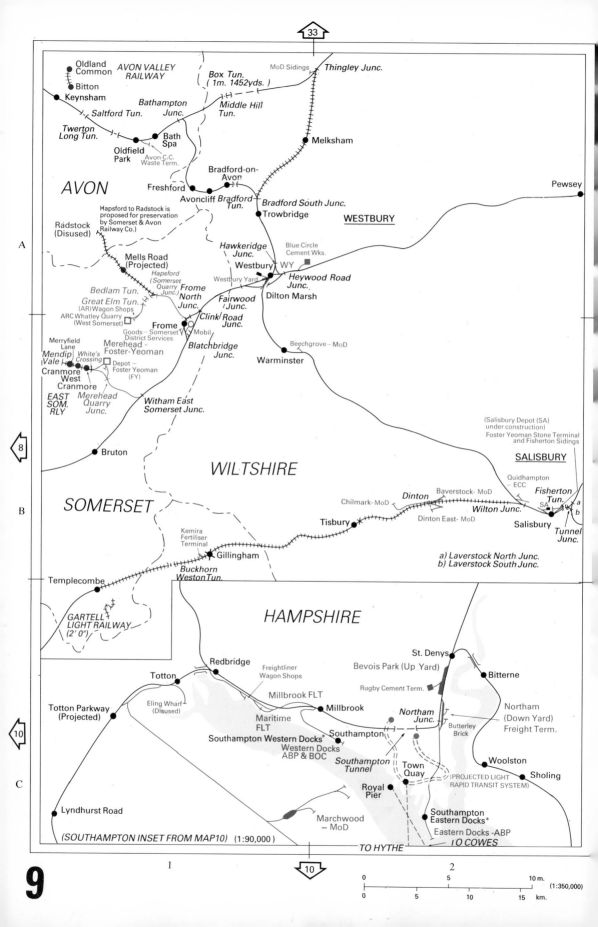

Oldland Common
Bitton
Keynsham
**AVON VALLEY RAILWAY**

MoD Sidings
Thingley Junc.

Box Tun.
(1m. 1452yds.)
Middle Hill Tun.
Saltford Tun.
Bathampton Junc.
Twerton Long Tun.
Oldfield Park
Bath Spa
Avon C.C. Waste Term.

Melksham

Bradford-on-Avon
Freshford
Avoncliff
Bradford Tun.
Bradford South Junc.
Trowbridge

**AVON**

Pewsey

**WESTBURY**

Radstock (Disused)

Hapsford to Radstock is proposed for preservation by Somerset & Avon Railway Co.)

Mells Road (Projected)

Hapsford (Somerset Quarry Junc.)
Bedlam Tun.
Great Elm Tun.
(AR)Wagon Shops
ARC Whatley Quarry (West Somerset)
Frome North Junc.
Clink Road Junc.
Frome
Goods – Somerset District Services
Mobil
Blatchbridge Junc.

*Hawkeridge Junc.*
Westbury
WY
Blue Circle Cement Wks.
Westbury Yard
Heywood Road Junc.
Dilton Marsh
Fairwood Junc.

A

Merryfield Lane
Mendip Vale
White's Crossing
Cranmore
West Cranmore
EAST SOM. RLY
Merehead Quarry Junc.
Merehead – Foster-Yeoman
Depot – Foster Yeoman (FY)
Witham East Somerset Junc.

Beechgrove – MoD
Warminster

8

Bruton

**WILTSHIRE**

(Salisbury Depot (SA) under construction)
Foster Yeoman Stone Terminal and Fisherton Sidings

**SALISBURY**

Quidhampton – ECC
Fisherton Tun.

**SOMERSET**

Chilmark- MoD
Dinton
Baverstock- MoD
Wilton Junc.
a
b
SA
Salisbury
Tunnel Junc.

B

Tisbury
Dinton East- MoD

Kemira Fertiliser Terminal

Gillingham
Buckhorn Weston Tun.

a) Laverstock North Junc.
b) Laverstock South Junc.

Templecombe

**HAMPSHIRE**

GARTELL LIGHT RAILWAY (2' 0")

Redbridge
Freightliner Wagon Shops
St. Denys
Bevois Park (Up Yard)
Bitterne

Totton
Rugby Cement Term.
Northam (Down Yard) Freight Term.

Totton Parkway (Projected)
Eling Wharf (Disused)
Millbrook FLT
Millbrook
Northam Junc.
Butterley Brick

10

Maritime FLT
Southampton
Woolston

Southampton Western Docks*
Western Docks ABP & BOC
Southampton Tunnel
Town Quay
Sholing
(PROJECTED LIGHT RAPID TRANSIT SYSTEM)

C

Royal Pier

Lyndhurst Road
Marchwood – MoD
Southampton Eastern Docks*
Eastern Docks -ABP
**I O COWES**

(SOUTHAMPTON INSET FROM MAP10) (1:90,000)

TO HYTHE

1

10

2

0    5    10 m.
(1:350,000)
0    5    10    15  km.

**9**

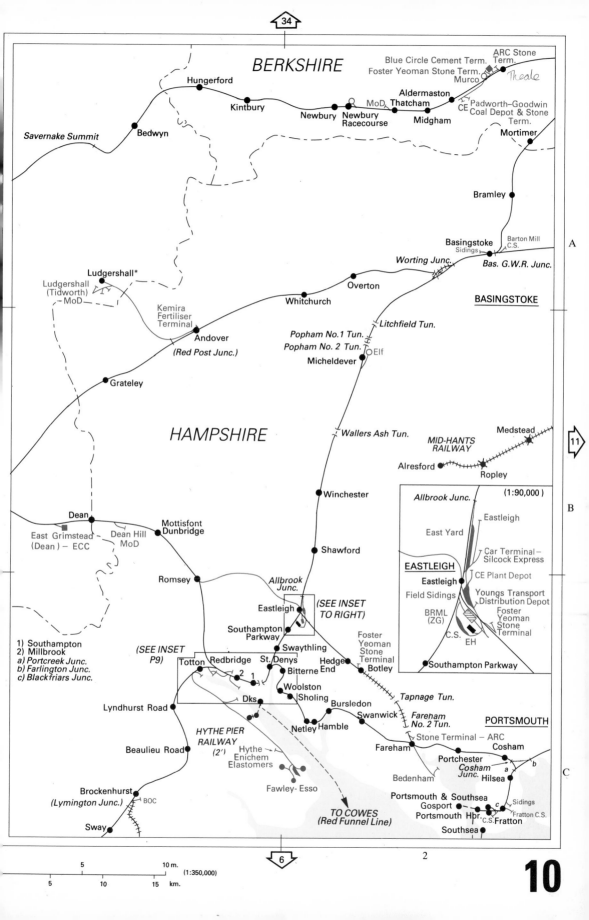

BERKSHIRE

Hungerford

Kintbury

Bedwyn

*Savernake Summit*

Newbury
Newbury
Racecourse

MoD Thatcham

Aldermaston

Midgham

Blue Circle Cement Term.
Foster Yeoman Stone Term.
Murco

ARC Stone
Term.

*Theale*

CE

Padworth–Goodwin
Coal Depot & Stone
Term.

Mortimer

Bramley

Basingstoke
Sidings

Barton Mill
C.S.

Bas. G.W.R. Junc.

A

*Worting Junc.*

BASINGSTOKE

Ludgershall*

Ludgershall
(Tidworth)
– MoD

Kemira
Fertiliser
Terminal

Andover

*(Red Post Junc.)*

Overton

Whitchurch

*Litchfield Tun.*

*Popham No.1 Tun.*
*Popham No.2 Tun.*

Micheldever

Elf

Grateley

HAMPSHIRE

*Wallers Ash Tun.*

MID-HANTS
RAILWAY

Medstead

11

Alresford

Ropley

B

Winchester

Dean

East Grimstead
(Dean) – ECC

Dean Hill
MoD

Mottisfont
Dunbridge

Shawford

(1:90,000)

*Allbrook Junc.*

Eastleigh

East Yard

EASTLEIGH

Eastleigh

Field Sidings

BRML
(ZG)

C.S.

EH

Car Terminal –
Silcock Express

CE Plant Depot

Youngs Transport
Distribution Depot

Foster
Yeoman
Stone
Terminal

Southampton Parkway

Romsey

*Allbrook
Junc.*

Eastleigh

*(SEE INSET
TO RIGHT)*

Southampton
Parkway

Swaythling

Hedge
End

Botley

Foster
Yeoman
Stone
Terminal

1) Southampton
2) Millbrook
a) Portcreek Junc.
b) Farlington Junc.
c) Blackfriars Junc.

*(SEE INSET
P9)*

Totton Redbridge

St. Denys

Bitterne

Woolston

Sholing

Dks

Lyndhurst Road

HYTHE PIER
RAILWAY
*(2')*

Hythe
Enichem
Elastomers

Fawley- Esso

Netley Hamble

Bursledon

Swanwick

*Tapnage Tun.*

*Fareham
No.2 Tun.*

Stone Terminal – ARC

Fareham

Bedenham

Portchester

*Cosham
Junc.*

Cosham

a

b

Hilsea

C

Beaulieu Road

Brockenhurst
(Lymington Junc.)

BOC

Sway

*TO COWES
(Red Funnel Line)*

Portsmouth & Southsea

Gosport

Portsmouth Hbr.

Southsea

c

C.S. Fratton

Sidings

Fratton C.S.

PORTSMOUTH

2

5        10 m.

(1:350,000)

5      10      15   km.

**10**

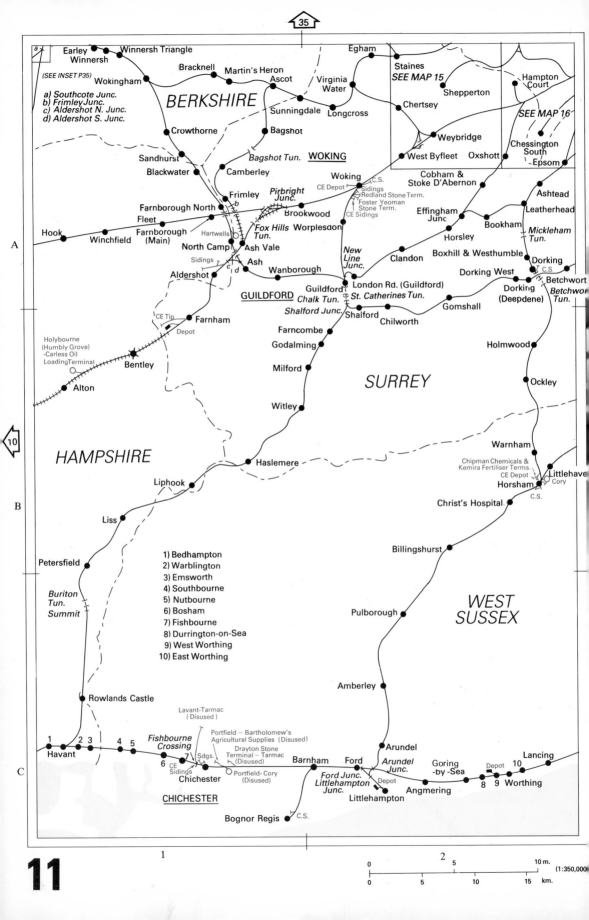

**11**

1    2    10 m.

0    5    10    15 km.

(1:350,000)

(SEE INSET P35)

a) Southcote Junc.
b) Frimley Junc.
c) Aldershot N. Junc.
d) Aldershot S. Junc.

Earley
Winnersh          Winnersh Triangle
Wokingham
Bracknell
Martin's Heron
Ascot
**BERKSHIRE**
Egham
Staines
*SEE MAP 15*
Shepperton
Hampton Court
*SEE MAP 16*

Virginia Water
Longcross
Chertsey
Weybridge
West Byfleet          Oxshott
Chessington South
Epsom

Crowthorne
Sunningdale
Bagshot
Sandhurst
Blackwater
*Bagshot Tun.*          **WOKING**
Camberley
Woking          C.S.
CE Depot          Sidings
Redland Stone Term.
Foster Yeoman
Stone Term.
CE Sidings

Cobham &
Stoke D'Abernon
Ashtead
Leatherhead

Frimley
*Pirbright Junc.*
Farnborough North
Fleet
Brookwood
Worplesdon
Effingham Junc.
Bookham
*Mickleham Tun.*

Hook
Winchfield
Farnborough (Main)
North Camp
Hartwells
*Fox Hills Tun.*
Ash Vale
Horsley
Boxhill & Westhumble
Dorking
C.S.
Betchworth

Sidings
Ash
Wanborough
*New Line Junc.*
Clandon
Dorking West
Dorking (Deepdene)
*Betchworth Tun.*

Aldershot
London Rd. (Guildford)
Guildford          St. Catherines Tun.
**GUILDFORD**
*Guildford Chalk Tun.*
Gomshall

CE Tip
Depot
Farnham
*Shalford Junc.*          Shalford
Chilworth
Holmwood

Holybourne
(Humbly Grove)
-Carless Oil
LoadingTerminal
Bentley
Farncombe
Godalming
Ockley

Alton
Milford
**SURREY**
Warnham

Witley
Chipman Chemicals &
Kemira Fertiliser Terms.
CE Depot          Littlehaven
Horsham          Cory
C.S.

**HAMPSHIRE**
Haslemere
Liphook
Christ's Hospital

Liss
Billingshurst

Petersfield
1) Bedhampton
2) Warblington
3) Emsworth
4) Southbourne
5) Nutbourne
6) Bosham
7) Fishbourne
8) Durrington-on-Sea
9) West Worthing
10) East Worthing

*Buriton Tun. Summit*
Pulborough
**WEST SUSSEX**

Amberley

Rowlands Castle

Lavant-Tarmac
( Disused )
Portfield – Bartholomew's
Agricultural Supplies (Disused)
1    2  3          4   5
*Fishbourne Crossing*
7    Sdgs.
Drayton Stone
Terminal – Tarmac
(Disused)
Barnham          Ford
Arundel
*Arundel Junc.*
Goring-by-Sea
Lancing
Depot          10

Havant
6    CE Sidings
Chichester
Portfield- Cory
(Disused)
Depot
*Ford Junc.*
*Littlehampton Junc.*
Angmering
8    9    Worthing

**CHICHESTER**
Littlehampton

Bognor Regis          C.S.

A

B

C

10

1                                    2

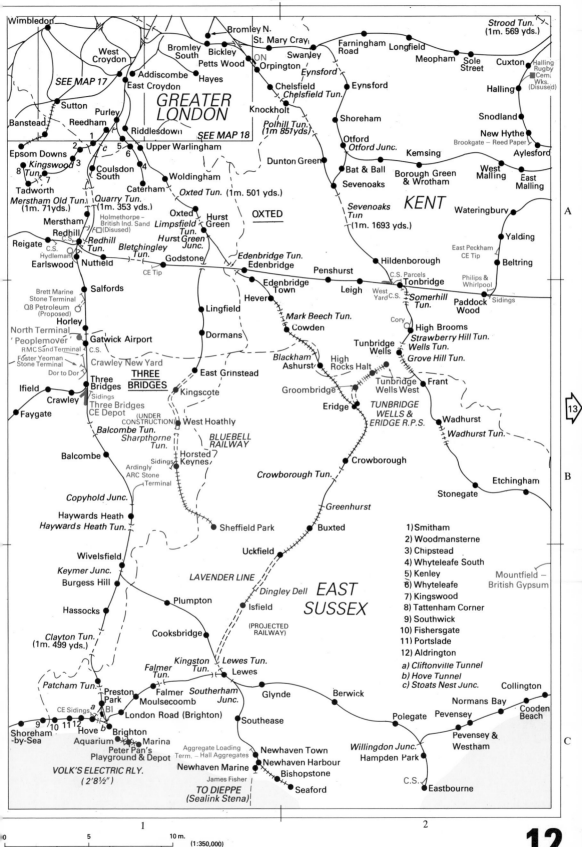

Wimbledon

Bromley N.

West
Croydon

Bromley
South  Bickley

St. Mary Cray

Farningham
Road   Longfield

Strood Tun.
(1m. 569 yds.)

Petts Wood

Meopham   Sole
Street   Cuxton

Halling
Rugby
Cem.
Wks.
(Disused)

SEE MAP 17

Addiscombe

Hayes

Orpington

ON

Swanley

Eynsford

Halling

East Croydon

Chelsfield

Eynsford

GREATER
LONDON

Sutton

Purley

Riddlesdown

Chelsfield Tun.

Snodland

Knockholt

Shoreham

New Hythe

Banstead

Reedham

SEE MAP 18

Polhill Tun.
(1m 857yds.)

Otford

Brookgate – Reed Paper

Upper Warlingham

Dunton Green

Otford Junc.

Kemsing

West
Malling  East
Malling

Aylesford

Epsom Downs

Kingswood
Tun.

Coulsdon
South

Woldingham

Bat & Ball

Borough Green
& Wrotham

Tadworth

Caterham

Sevenoaks

KENT

Oxted Tun. (1m. 501 yds.)

Wateringbury

Merstham Old Tun.
(1m. 71yds.)  Quarry Tun.
(1m. 353 yds.)

Oxted   Hurst
Green

OXTED

Sevenoaks
Tun.
(1m. 1693 yds.)

Yalding

Merstham

Holmethorpe –
British Ind. Sand
(Disused)

Limpsfield
Tun.

Hurst Green
Junc.

East Peckham
CE Tip

Redhill

C.S.

Redhill
Tun.  Bletchingley
Tun.

Godstone

Edenbridge Tun.
Edenbridge

Hildenborough

Beltring

Reigate   C.S.
Hydleman

Earlswood  Nutfield

CE Tip

Penshurst

C.S. Parcels

Tonbridge

Philips &
Whirlpool

Salfords

Edenbridge
Town   Leigh

West
Yard C.S.  Somerhill
Tun.

Sidings

Horley

Lingfield

Hever

Paddock
Wood

Brett Marine
Stone Terminal
Q8 Petroleum
(Proposed)

Mark Beech Tun.

Cowden

Cory

High Brooms

Strawberry Hill Tun.

North Terminal
'Peoplemover'
RMC Sand Terminal  C.S.

Gatwick Airport

Dormans

Tunbridge
Wells  Wells Tun.

Grove Hill Tun.

Foster Yeoman
Stone Terminal
Dor to Dor

Crawley New Yard

Blackham
Ashurst

High
Rocks Halt

Tunbridge
Wells West

Frant

Ifield

THREE
BRIDGES

East Grinstead

Groombridge

TUNBRIDGE
WELLS &
ERIDGE R.P.S.

Crawley

Three
Bridges  Sidings

Kingscote

Eridge

Wadhurst

Faygate

Three Bridges
CE Depot  (UNDER
CONSTRUCTION)  West Hoathly

Wadhurst Tun.

Balcombe Tun.
Sharpthorne
Tun.

BLUEBELL
RAILWAY

Balcombe

Ardingly
ARC Stone
Terminal

Horsted
Keynes

Sidings

Crowborough

Etchingham

Copyhold Junc.

Crowborough Tun.

Stonegate

Haywards Heath
Haywards Heath Tun.

Sheffield Park

Buxted

Greenhurst

1) Smitham

Wivelsfield

Uckfield

2) Woodmansterne

Keymer Junc.
Burgess Hill

LAVENDER LINE

EAST
SUSSEX

3) Chipstead

4) Whyteleafe South

Mountfield –
British Gypsum

Hassocks

Plumpton

Dingley Dell

5) Kenley

6) Whyteleafe

Clayton Tun.
(1m. 499 yds.)

Cooksbridge

Isfield

(PROJECTED
RAILWAY)

7) Kingswood

8) Tattenham Corner

9) Southwick

Kingston
Tun.

Lewes Tun.

10) Fishersgate

Falmer
Tun.

Lewes

11) Portslade

Patcham Tun.

Preston
Park

Falmer

Moulsecoomb

Southerham
Junc.

Glynde

Berwick

Normans Bay

12) Aldrington

a) Cliftonville Tunnel
b) Hove Tunnel
c) Stoats Nest Junc.

Collington

CE Sidings  a   B1

London Road (Brighton)

Southease

Polegate

Pevensey

Cooden
Beach

Shoreham
-by-Sea

Hove

Brighton

Aquarium

Marina

Willingdon Junc.

Pevensey &
Westham

Peter Pan's
Playground & Depot

Aggregate Loading
Term. – Hall Aggregates

Newhaven Town

Hampden Park

VOLK'S ELECTRIC RLY.
(2'8½")

Newhaven Harbour

Bishopstone

C.S.

Newhaven Marine

James Fisher

Seaford

Eastbourne

TO DIEPPE
(Sealink Stena)

A

13

B

C

1

2

0   5   10 m.

(1:350,000)

0   5   10   15   km.

**12**

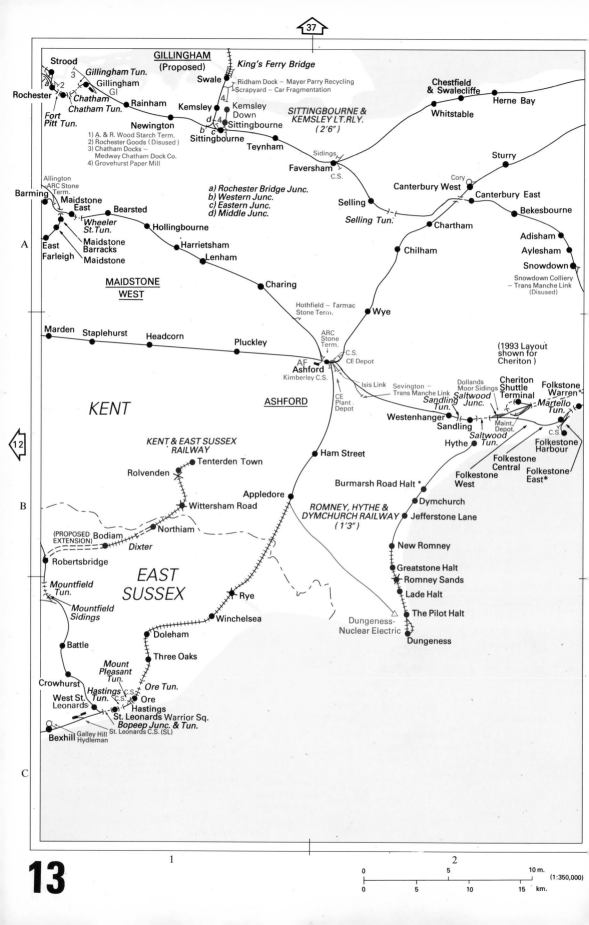

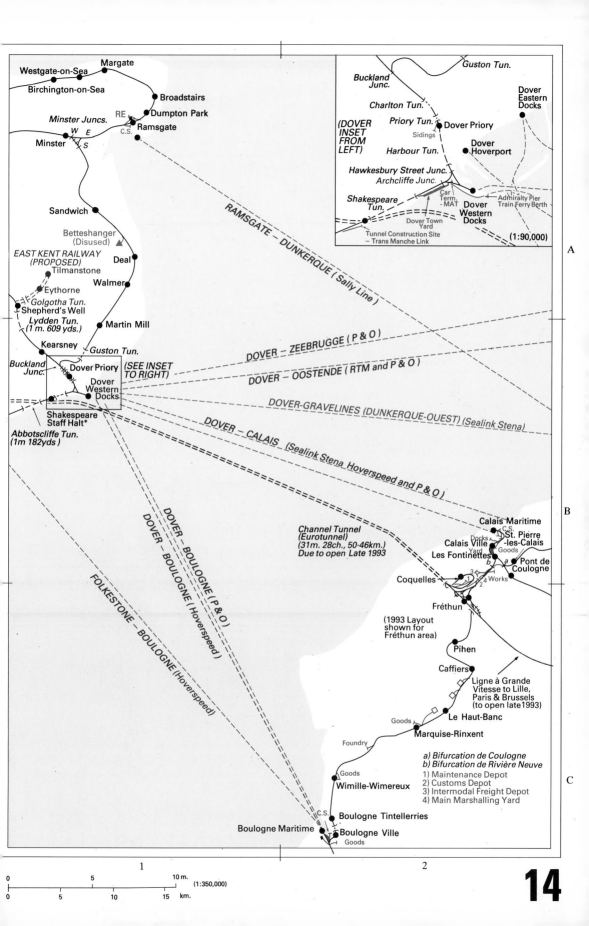

Margate
Westgate-on-Sea
Birchington-on-Sea
Minster Juncs.       RE
Minster       W   E       Ramsgate
              S       C.S.
                     Dumpton Park
                     Broadstairs

Sandwich

Betteshanger
(Disused)
EAST KENT RAILWAY
(PROPOSED)       Deal
Tilmanstone
Eythorne       Walmer
Golgotha Tun.
Shepherd's Well       Martin Mill
Lydden Tun.
(1 m. 609 yds.)
Kearsney       Guston Tun.
Buckland       Dover Priory       (SEE INSET
Junc.                             TO RIGHT)
              Dover
              Western
              Docks
Shakespeare
Staff Halt*
Abbotscliffe Tun.
(1m 182yds )

RAMSGATE – DUNKERQUE ( Sally Line )

DOVER – ZEEBRUGGE ( P & O )
DOVER – OOSTENDE ( RTM and P & O )
DOVER–GRAVELINES (DUNKERQUE-OUEST) (Sealink Stena)
DOVER – CALAIS  (Sealink Stena Hoverspeed and P & O)

DOVER – BOULOGNE ( P & O )
DOVER – BOULOGNE (Hoverspeed)
FOLKESTONE – BOULOGNE (Hoverspeed)

Channel Tunnel
(Eurotunnel)
(31m. 28ch., 50·46km.)
Due to open Late 1993

**A**

(DOVER
INSET
FROM
LEFT)

Guston Tun.
Buckland
Junc.
Charlton Tun.
Priory Tun.       Dover Priory
       Sidings
Harbour Tun.       Dover
                  Hoverport
Hawkesbury Street Junc.
Archcliffe Junc.
Shakespeare       Car
Tun.              Term.
                  - MAT       Dover
                              Western
       Dover Town              Docks
       Yard
Tunnel Construction Site
– Trans Manche Link       (1:90,000)

Dover
Eastern
Docks

Admiralty Pier
Train Ferry Berth

**B**

Calais Maritime
              C.S.
       Docks       St. Pierre
Calais Ville              -les-Calais
       Yard       Goods
Les Fontinettes
                  b       Pont de
              a           Coulogne
Coquelles       3
              2  4  Works
Fréthun

(1993 Layout
shown for
Fréthun area)

Pihen

Caffiers
       Ligne à Grande
       Vitesse to Lille,
       Paris & Brussels
       (to open late1993)
Goods
       Le Haut-Banc
Marquise-Rinxent
Foundry

Goods

Wimille-Wimereux

              C.S.
Boulogne Maritime       Boulogne Tintellerries
                        Boulogne Ville
                        Goods

a) Bifurcation de Coulogne
b) Bifurcation de Rivière Neuve
1) Maintenance Depot
2) Customs Depot
3) Intermodal Freight Depot
4) Main Marshalling Yard

**C**

1       2

0       5       10 m.
                (1:350,000)
0    5      10      15   km.

**14**

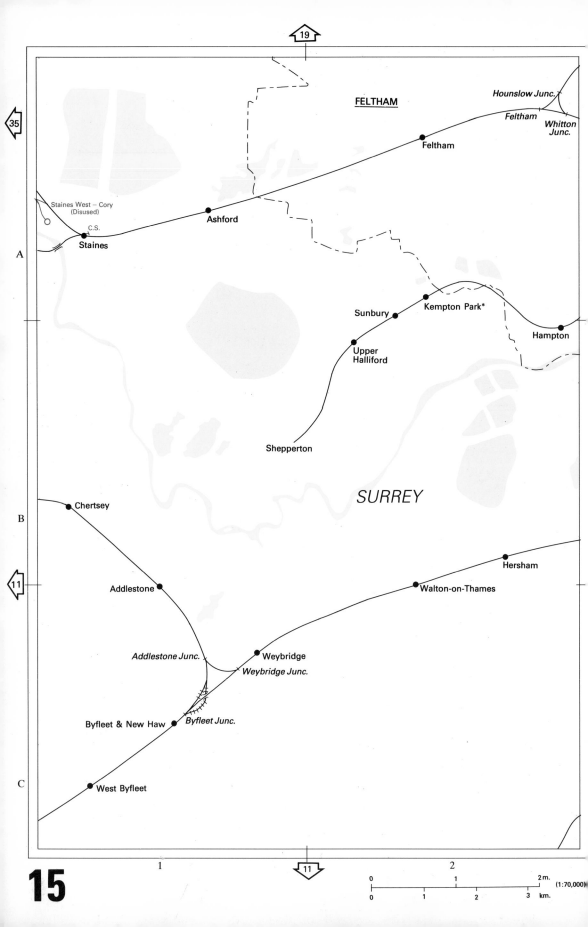

**FELTHAM**

*Hounslow Junc.*

Feltham

*Feltham*

*Whitton Junc.*

Staines West – Cory
(Disused)

C.S.

**Staines**

**Ashford**

A

Sunbury

Kempton Park*

Hampton

Upper
Halliford

Shepperton

*SURREY*

Chertsey

B

Hersham

Addlestone

Walton-on-Thames

*Addlestone Junc.*

Weybridge

*Weybridge Junc.*

Byfleet & New Haw

*Byfleet Junc.*

C

West Byfleet

**15**

1

2

0        1        2 m.

0      1      2      3 km.

(1:70,000)

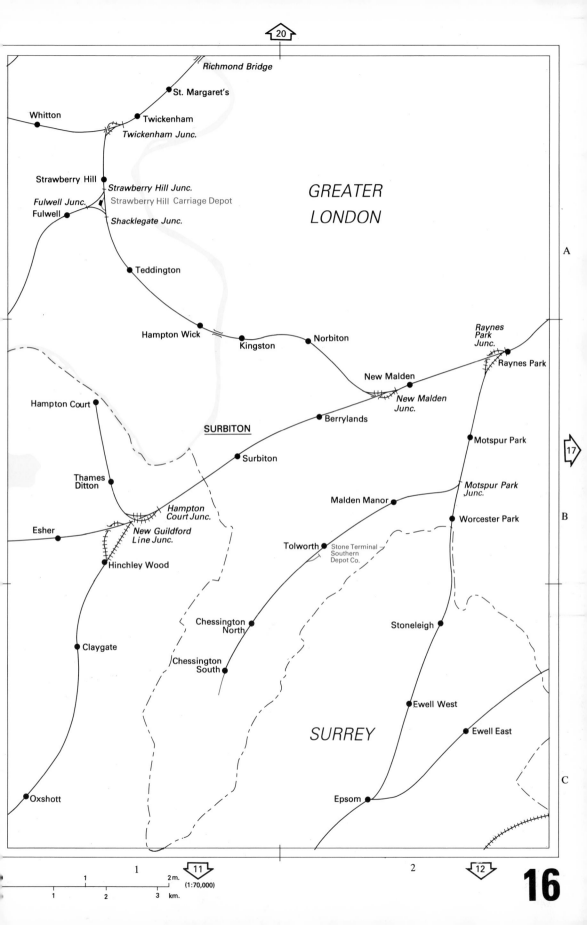

East Putney Tun.
D
Southfields
D
Earlsfield
Wandsworth Common
Balham
Clapham South
Wimbledon Park
WD
Wimbledon Staff Halt*
**WIMBLEDON**
Balham Junc.
N
Tooting Bec
Tooting Broadway
Balham
C.S. & E.M.U. Depot
Streatham Hill
Leigham Junc.
Leigham Court (Streatham Hill) Tun.
Leigham Tun.
Herne Hill N. Junc.
Herne Hill
Herne Hill S. Junc.
North Dulwich
Knight's Hill Tunnel
Tulse Hill
West Dulwich
West Norwood Junc.
West Norwood
Sydenham Hill
Penge Tunnel (1m. 381 yds )
Gipsy Hill

A
Haydons Road
'B' Junc.
'A' Junc. Wimbledon
Wimbledon S & T Depot
Collier's Wood
South Wimbledon
Tooting
Streatham Junc. North
Streatham
Streatham Junc. S.
Streatham Tun.
Streatham Common
Crystal Palace Tun.
Crystal Palace

'C' Junc.
Merton Park
Wimbledon Chase
N
South Merton
Morden Road
Morden
Depot
Morden South
St. Helier
Eastfields (Proposed)
Streatham Common Junc.
Norbury
**GREATER LONDON**
Thornton Heath
Bromley Junc.
Norwood Junction
Norwood Junc.
Selhurst Depot
SU
Selhurst
Selhurst Junc.
Gloucester Rd. Junc.
Cottage Junc.
Norwood Fork Junc.
Norwood Yard

Mitcham
Mitcham North Junc.
Mitcham Junction
Mitcham South Junc.
Beddington Lane
Windmill Bridge Junc.

B
Sutton Common
Hackbridge
Waddon Marsh
West Croydon
East Croydon
Addiscombe
Depot

West Sutton
Carshalton
Waddon
South Croydon
South Croydon Junc.
Selsdon – Cory
Selsdon Junc.

Cheam
Sutton Junc.
Sutton
Sutton Wimbledon Line Junc.
Ventnor Road
Wallington
Carshalton Beeches
Sanderstead
Purley Oaks

Belmont
Stone Terminal- Foster Yeoman
Purley
Caterham Line Junc.
Stone Terminal – Brett Marine
Riddlesdown

C
Reedham
Chipstead Line Junc.
Riddlesdown Tunnel
**SURREY**
Banstead
Kenley

16

**17**

1
| | | | |
|---|---|---|---|
| B | BAKERLOO | M | METROPOLITAN |
| C | CENTRAL | M(EL) | METROPOLITAN (East London) |
| O | CIRCLE | N | NORTHERN |
| D | DISTRICT | P | PICCADILLY |
| J | JUBILEE | V | VICTORIA |

2
0    1    2 m.
0  1  2  3 km.
(1:70,00

Hither Green
*Lee Junc.*
Lee
HG
CE Plant Depot
*Lee Spur Junc.*
Honor Oak Park
Crofton Park
Catford
Catford Bridge
Hither Green Freight Yard
Mottingham
New Eltham
36
Forest Hill
Bellingham
Hither Green C.S.
E.M.U. Depot
Grove Park
*Grove Park Junc.*
Sydenham
Lower Sydenham
Beckenham Hill
*Chislehurst Tunnels*
Elmstead Woods
A
*Sydenham Junc.*
Penge East
Penge West
New Beckenham
*New Beckenham Junc.*
Beckenham Junction
Ravensbourne
Sundridge Park
Bromley North
ARC Stone Term.
Chislehurst
Anerley
Kent House
Clock House
*Shortlands Junc.*
*Bickley Junc.*
*Chislehurst Junc.*
Birkbeck
Shortlands
Bromley South
Bickley
St. Mary Cray Junc.
Elmers End
*Elmers End Junc.*
*Petts Wood Junc.*
B
Eden Park
Petts Wood
Woodside
West Wickham
12

(Projected 'Tramlink' network
shown. BR services from
Elmers End to Addiscombe,
West Croydon to Wimbledon and
Birkbeck to Beckenham would
be replaced by Tramlink)

Hayes

*GREATER  LONDON*

New Addington

C

*SURREY*

1                                    2
0        1        2 m.
0    1    2    3  km.
(1:70,000)

**18**

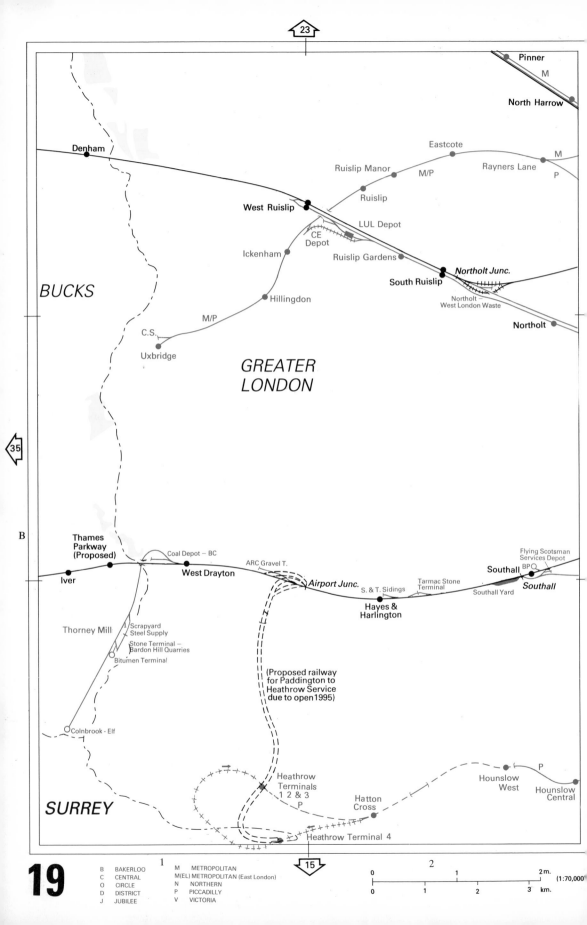

Pinner
M
North Harrow

Eastcote
Ruislip Manor
M/P
Rayners Lane
M
P

West Ruislip
Ruislip
LUL Depot
CE Depot
Ruislip Gardens
*Northolt Junc.*
South Ruislip

Ickenham
Northolt
West London Waste
Northolt

*BUCKS*

Hillingdon
M/P

C.S.
Uxbridge

*GREATER LONDON*

Denham

B

Thames Parkway (Proposed)
Coal Depot – BC
ARC Gravel T.
Flying Scotsman Services Depot
Southall
BPQ
Iver
West Drayton
Airport Junc.
S. & T. Sidings
Tarmac Stone Terminal
Southall Yard
*Southall*
Hayes & Harlington

Thorney Mill
Scrapyard Steel Supply
Stone Terminal – Bardon Hill Quarries
Bitumen Terminal

(Proposed railway for Paddington to Heathrow Service due to open 1995)

Colnbrook - Elf

Heathrow Terminals 1 2 & 3
P
Hatton Cross
Hounslow West
P
Hounslow Central

*SURREY*

Heathrow Terminal 4

# 19

1

| B | BAKERLOO | M | METROPOLITAN |
| C | CENTRAL | M(EL) | METROPOLITAN (East London) |
| O | CIRCLE | N | NORTHERN |
| D | DISTRICT | P | PICCADILLY |
| J | JUBILEE | V | VICTORIA |

2

0                    1                    2 m.

(1:70,000)

0          1          2          3 km.

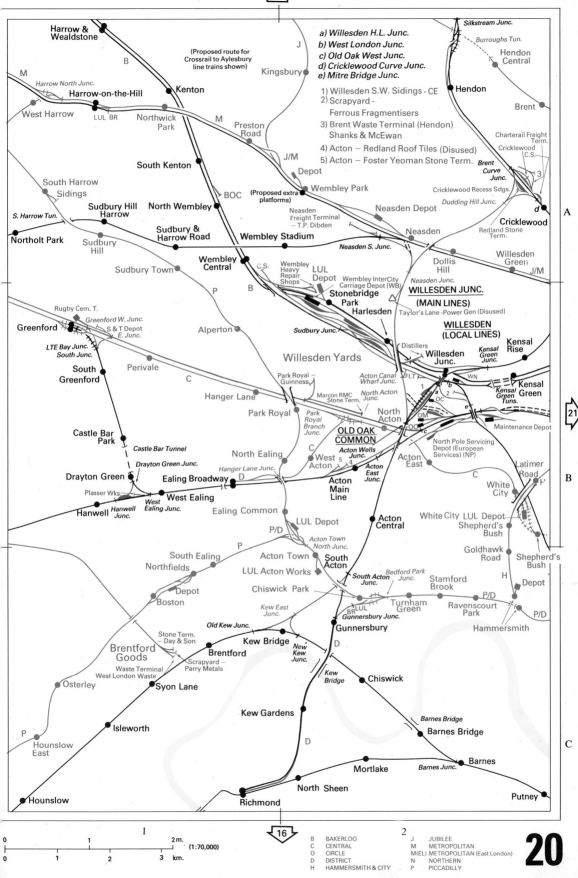

a) Willesden H.L. Junc.
b) West London Junc.
c) Old Oak West Junc.
d) Cricklewood Curve Junc.
e) Mitre Bridge Junc.

1) Willesden S.W. Sidings - CE
2) Scrapyard -
Ferrous Fragmentisers
3) Brent Waste Terminal (Hendon)
Shanks & McEwan
4) Acton — Redland Roof Tiles (Disused)
5) Acton — Foster Yeoman Stone Term.

Harrow & Wealdstone
Harrow North Junc.
M
Harrow-on-the-Hill
West Harrow
LUL  BR
Kenton
Northwick Park
M
J
Kingsbury
Preston Road
J/M
Silkstream Junc.
Burroughs Tun.
Hendon Central
Hendon
Brent
Charterail Freight Term.
Cricklewood C.S.
Brent Curve Junc.
Cricklewood
d
A
Cricklewood Recess Sdgs.
Dudding Hill Junc.
Redland Stone Term.

(Proposed route for Crossrail to Aylesbury line trains shown)

South Harrow Sidings
Sudbury Hill Harrow
North Wembley
S. Harrow Tun.
Northolt Park
Sudbury Hill
Sudbury & Harrow Road
Sudbury Town
Depot
Wembley Park
(Proposed extra platforms)
BOC
Wembley Stadium
Neasden Freight Terminal – T.P. Dibden
Neasden Depot
Neasden
Neasden S. Junc.
Dollis Hill
Willesden Green
J/M

Wembley Central
Wembley Heavy Repair Shops
LUL Depot
Stonebridge Park
Harlesden
C.S.
B
Neasden Junc.
Wembley InterCity Carriage Depot (WB)
WILLESDEN JUNC.
(MAIN LINES)
Taylor's Lane -Power Gen (Disused)
WILLESDEN (LOCAL LINES)

Rugby Cem. T.
Greenford W. Junc.
S & T Depot
E. Junc.
Greenford
LTE Bay Junc.
South Junc.
South Greenford
Perivale
P
Alperton
Hanger Lane
C
Park Royal Guinness
Park Royal
Sudbury Junc.
Willesden Yards
Marcon RMC Stone Term.
North Acton Junc.
Park Royal Branch Junc.
Acton Canal Wharf Junc.
North Acton
Distillers
FLT
1
a b
OC
Willesden Junc.
Kensal Green Junc.
Kensal Rise
Kensal Green
Kensal Green Tuns.
WN
2
e
OO
Maintenance Depot
21

Castle Bar Park
Castle Bar Tunnel
Drayton Green Junc.
Drayton Green
Plasser Wks.
Hanwell
Hanwell Junc.
West Ealing
West Ealing Junc.
North Ealing
Ealing Broadway
D
West Acton
C
Hanger Lane Junc.
Acton Wells Junc.
OLD OAK COMMON
5
4
Acton Main Line
Acton East Junc.
Acton East
North Pole Servicing Depot (European Services) (NP)
OM
c
B
Latimer Road
White City
C
White City LUL Depot
Shepherd's Bush

Ealing Common
LUL Depot
P/D
P
Acton Town North Junc.
South Ealing
Northfields
Acton Town
LUL Acton Works
South Acton
South Acton Junc.
Chiswick Park
Acton Central
Bedford Park Junc.
Stamford Brook
Goldhawk Road
Shepherd's Bush
H
Depot
P/D

Depot
Boston
Kew East Junc.
BR LUL
Gunnersbury Junc.
Turnham Green
Ravenscourt Park
P/D
Hammersmith
P/D

Stone Term. – Day & Son
Old Kew Junc.
Brentford Goods
Brentford
Waste Terminal West London Waste
Scrapyard – Parry Metals
Kew Bridge
New Kew Junc.
Gunnersbury
Kew Bridge
D
Chiswick
Osterley
Syon Lane
Kew Gardens
Barnes Bridge
Barnes Bridge
Hounslow East
P
Isleworth
D
Mortlake
Barnes Junc.
Barnes
C
Hounslow
North Sheen
Richmond
Putney

0    1    2 m.    (1:70,000)
0    1    2    3 km.

B    BAKERLOO
C    CENTRAL
O    CIRCLE
D    DISTRICT
H    HAMMERSMITH & CITY
J    JUBILEE
M    METROPOLITAN
M(EL)    METROPOLITAN (East London)
N    NORTHERN
P    PICCADILLY

**20**

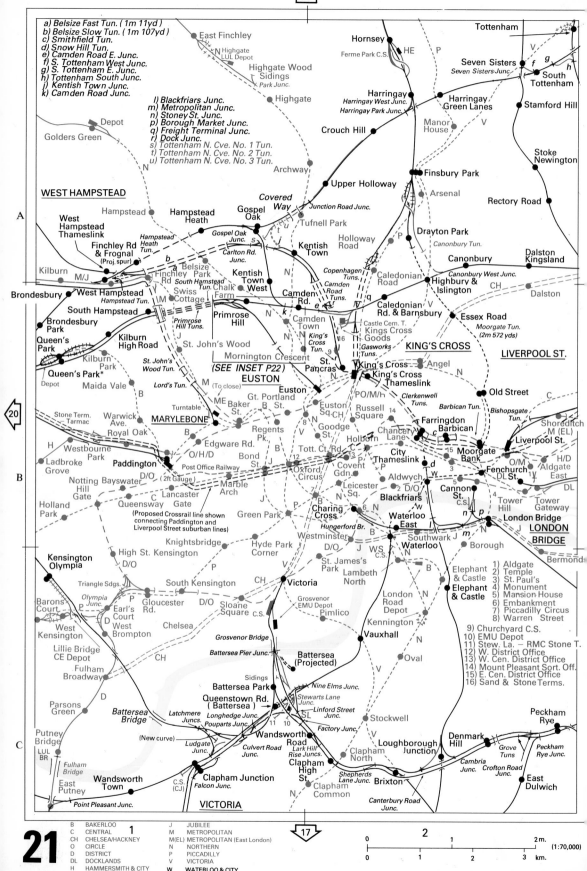

a) Belsize Fast Tun. ( 1m 11yd )
b) Belsize Slow Tun. ( 1m 107yd )
c) Smithfield Tun.
d) Snow Hill Tun.
e) Camden Road E. Junc.
f) S. Tottenham West Junc.
g) S. Tottenham E. Junc.
h) Tottenham South Junc.
i) Kentish Town Junc.
k) Camden Road Junc.

l) Blackfriars Junc.
m) Metropolitan Junc.
n) Stoney St. Junc.
p) Borough Market Junc.
q) Freight Terminal Junc.
r) Dock Junc.
s) Tottenham N. Cve. No. 1 Tun.
t) Tottenham N. Cve. No. 2 Tun.
u) Tottenham N. Cve. No. 3 Tun.

Tottenham
East Finchley
Hornsey
Seven Sisters
Seven Sisters Junc.
South Tottenham
Stamford Hill
Ferme Park C.S.
HE
Highgate LUL Depot
Highgate Wood Sidings
Park Junc.
Highgate
Harringay
Harringay West Junc.
Harringay Park Junc.
Harringay Green Lanes
Stoke Newington
Manor House
Crouch Hill
Rectory Road
Archway
Upper Holloway
Finsbury Park
Arsenal
WEST HAMPSTEAD
West Hampstead
Hampstead
Hampstead Heath
Gospel Oak
Covered Way
Junction Road Junc.
Tufnell Park
Drayton Park
Golders Green
Depot
Gospel Oak Junc.
Holloway Road
Canonbury Tun.
West Hampstead Thameslink
Hampstead Heath Tun.
Kentish Town
Carlton Rd. Junc.
Dalston Kingsland
Finchley Rd & Frognal (Proj. spur)
Finchley Rd
Belsize Park
South Hampstead Tun.
Chalk Farm
Kentish Town West
Copenhagen Tuns.
Camden Road Tuns.
Caledonian Road
Highbury & Islington
Canonbury West Junc.
Canonbury
Dalston
Kilburn
M/J
Swiss Cottage
Camden Rd.
Camden Road Junc.
Caledonian Rd. & Barnsbury
CH
Brondesbury
West Hampstead
Hampstead Tun.
South Hampstead
Primrose Hill Tuns.
Camden Town
Essex Road
Moorgate Tun. (2m 572 yds)
Brondesbury Park
Primrose Hill
King's Cross Junc.
Castle Cem. T.
Kings Cross Goods
KING'S CROSS
Queen's Park
Kilburn High Road
St. John's Wood
Mornington Crescent
King's Cross
Gasworks Tuns.
LIVERPOOL ST.
Queen's Park*
Kilburn Park
St. John's Wood Tun.
(SEE INSET P22)
EUSTON
(To close)
St. Pancras
King's Cross Thameslink
Angel
Old Street
Depot
Maida Vale
Lord's Tun.
M
Euston
Clerkenwell Tuns.
C
Warwick Ave.
Stone Term. Tarmac
ME
Baker St.
Gt. Portland St.
Euston Sq.
CH
Russell Square
PO/M/h
Barbican Tun.
Bishopsgate Tun.
Shoreditch M (EL)
Royal Oak
MARYLEBONE
Regents Pk.
Goodge St.
Farringdon
Barbican
Moorgate Bank
Liverpool St.
Westbourne Park
Edgware Rd.
O/H/D
Bond St.
Tott. Ct. Rd.
Holborn
Chancery Lane
c
Ladbroke Grove
Paddington
D/O
Post Office Railway (2ft Gauge)
Oxford Circus
Covent Gdn.
City Thameslink
Aldwych
d
w
Fenchurch DL St.
O/M
H/D
Aldgate East
DL
Notting Hill Gate
Bayswater
Marble Arch
Leicester Sq.
Blackfriars
Cannon St.
Holland Park
Lancaster Gate
Queensway
(Proposed Crossrail line shown connecting Paddington and Liverpool Street suburban lines)
Green Park
Charing Cross
Waterloo East
n
p
C.S.
Tower Hill
Tower Gateway
London Bridge
LONDON BRIDGE
Hungerford Br.
Southwark
Borough
Bermond
Westminster
Kensington Olympia
High St. Kensington
D/O
Hyde Park Corner
D/O
Waterloo
St. James's Park
Lambeth North
WS
m
J
Triangle Sdgs.
Olympia Junc.
South Kensington
CH
Victoria
Elephant & Castle
Elephant & Castle
London Road Depot
Barons Court
Earl's Court
Gloucester Rd.
D/O
Sloane Square
Grosvenor EMU Depot
Pimlico
1) Aldgate
2) Temple
3) St. Paul's
4) Monument
5) Mansion House
6) Embankment
7) Piccadilly Circus
8) Warren Street
West Kensington
West Brompton
Chelsea
C.S.
Kennington
9) Churchyard C.S.
10) EMU Depot
11) Stew. La. – RMC Stone T.
12) W. District Office
13) W. Cen. District Office
14) Mount Pleasant Sort. Off.
15) E. Cen. District Office
16) Sand & Stone Terms.
Lillie Bridge CE Depot
Fulham Broadway
Grosvenor Bridge
Battersea Pier Junc.
Battersea (Projected)
Vauxhall
Parsons Green
Sidings
Battersea Park
Oval
Putney Bridge
LUL BR
Fulham Bridge
Battersea Bridge
Queenstown Rd. (Battersea)
Latchmere Juncs.
Longhedge Junc.
Pouparts Junc.
Nine Elms Junc.
Stewarts Lane Junc.
Linford Street Junc.
SL
Stockwell
Peckham Rye
Denmark Hill
Grove Tuns
Peckham Rye Junc.
East Putney
(New curve)
Ludgate Junc.
Culvert Road Junc.
Lark Hill Rise Juncs.
Factory Junc.
Loughborough Junction
Cambria Junc.
Crofton Road Junc.
Wandsworth Town
C.S. (CJ)
Falcon Junc.
Clapham Junction
Wandsworth Road
Clapham High St.
Clapham North
Shepherds Lane Junc.
Brixton
East Dulwich
Point Pleasant Junc.
VICTORIA
Clapham Common
Canterbury Road Junc.

**21**

| B | BAKERLOO | | J | JUBILEE |
|---|---|---|---|---|
| C | CENTRAL | **1** | M | METROPOLITAN |
| CH | CHELSEA/HACKNEY | | M(EL) | METROPOLITAN (East London) |
| O | CIRCLE | | N | NORTHERN |
| D | DISTRICT | | P | PICCADILLY |
| DL | DOCKLANDS | | V | VICTORIA |
| H | HAMMERSMITH & CITY | | **W** | **WATERLOO & CITY** |

0    2    2m.
0    1    2    3 km.
(1:70,000)

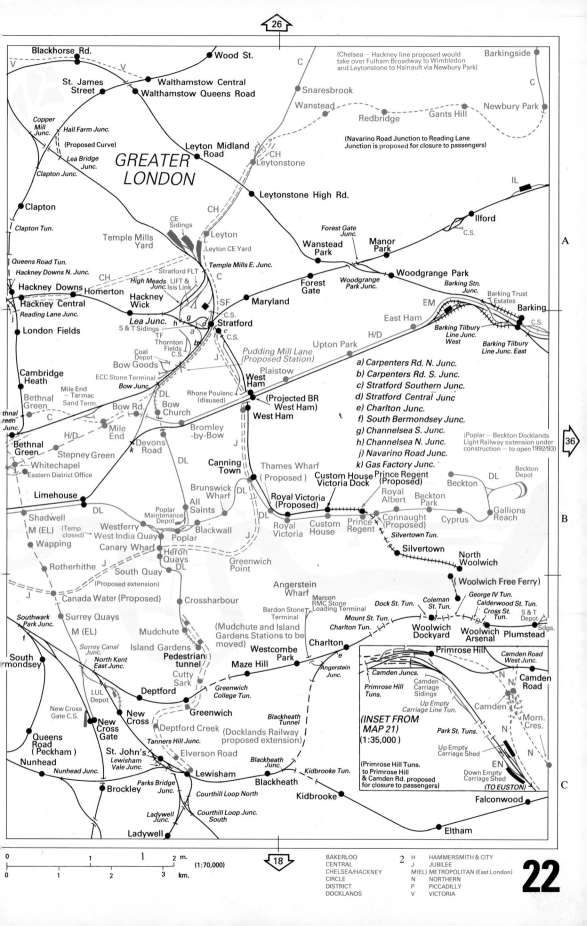

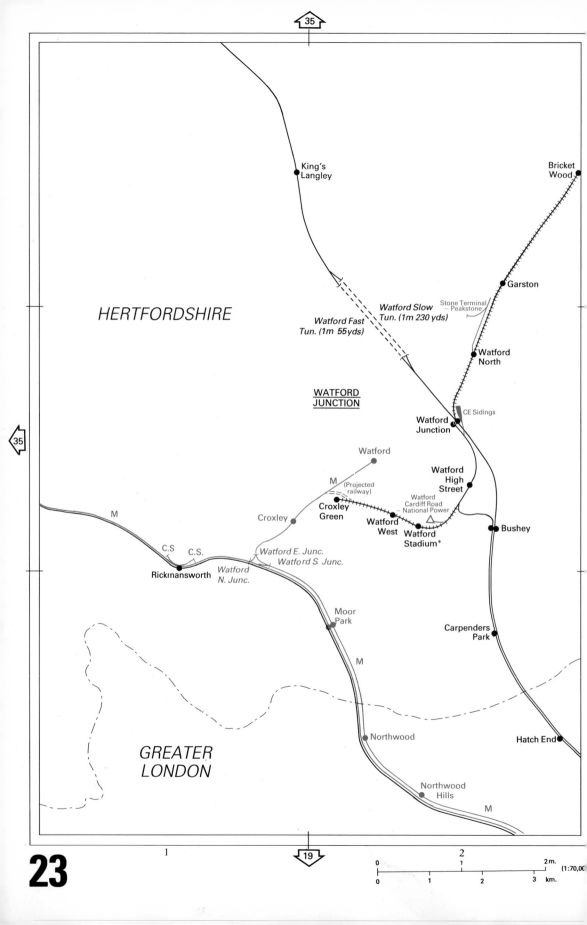

King's
Langley

Bricket
Wood

HERTFORDSHIRE

Garston

*Watford Fast
Tun. (1m 55 yds)*

Stone Terminal
— Peakstone

*Watford Slow
Tun. (1m 230 yds)*

Watford
North

WATFORD
JUNCTION

CE Sidings

Watford
Junction

Watford

Watford
High
Street

M

*(Projected
railway)*

Croxley

Croxley
Green

Watford
Cardiff Road
National Power

M

Watford
West

Watford
Stadium*

Bushey

C.S

C.S.

*Watford E. Junc.*
*Watford S. Junc.*

Rickmansworth

*Watford
N. Junc.*

Moor
Park

Carpenders
Park

M

GREATER
LONDON

Northwood

Hatch End

Northwood
Hills

M

23

0       1       2 m.

0     1     2     3   km.

(1:70,00

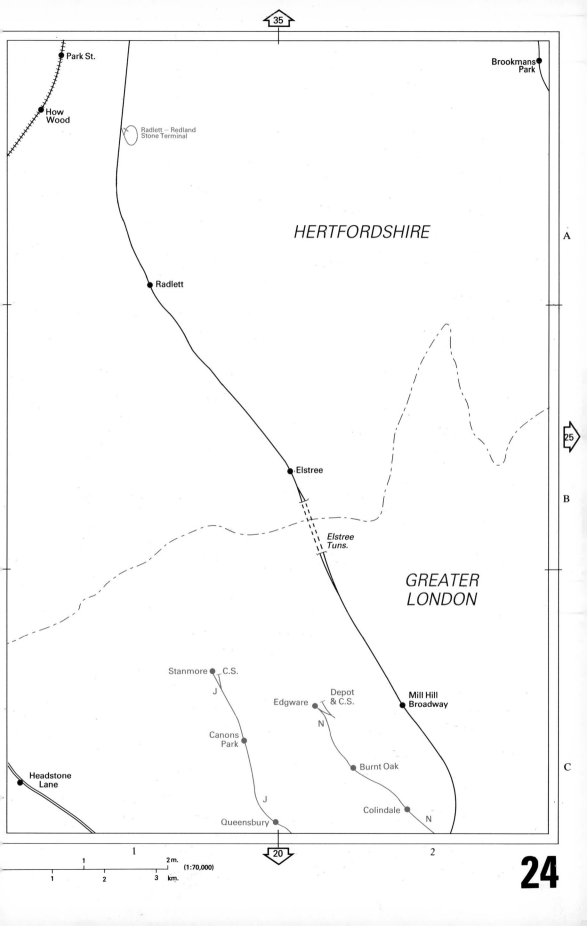

35

Park St.

Brookmans
Park

How
Wood

Radlett — Redland
Stone Terminal

HERTFORDSHIRE

A

Radlett

25

Elstree

B

Elstree
Tuns.

GREATER
LONDON

Stanmore • C.S.

J

Depot
& C.S.

Mill Hill
Broadway

Edgware

N

Canons
Park

Headstone
Lane

Burnt Oak

C

J

Colindale

N

Queensbury

1        2 m.
1
1        2
1        2        3   km.

(1:70,000)

20

2

**24**

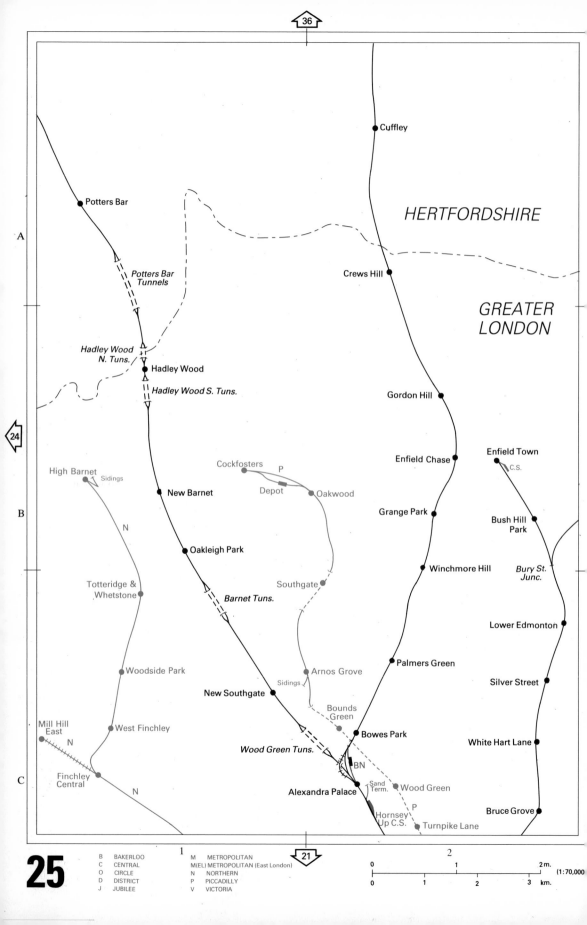

Cuffley

*HERTFORDSHIRE*

Potters Bar

A

*Potters Bar Tunnels*

Crews Hill

*GREATER LONDON*

*Hadley Wood N. Tuns.*

Hadley Wood

*Hadley Wood S. Tuns.*

Gordon Hill

24

Enfield Chase

Enfield Town

C.S.

Cockfosters

P

New Barnet

Depot

Oakwood

High Barnet

Sidings

Grange Park

Bush Hill Park

B

N

Oakleigh Park

Winchmore Hill

*Bury St. Junc.*

Totteridge & Whetstone

Southgate

*Barnet Tuns.*

Lower Edmonton

Palmers Green

Woodside Park

Silver Street

New Southgate

Arnos Grove

Sidings

Mill Hill East

West Finchley

Bounds Green

Bowes Park

White Hart Line

N

BN

*Wood Green Tuns.*

Finchley Central

Sand Term.

Wood Green

C

N

Alexandra Palace

Bruce Grove

Hornsey Up C.S.

P

Turnpike Lane

**25**

| B | BAKERLOO | M | METROPOLITAN |
|---|---|---|---|
| C | CENTRAL | M(EL) | METROPOLITAN (East London) |
| O | CIRCLE | N | NORTHERN |
| D | DISTRICT | P | PICCADILLY |
| J | JUBILEE | V | VICTORIA |

2

0        1        2 m.

0    1    2    3    km.

(1:70,000)

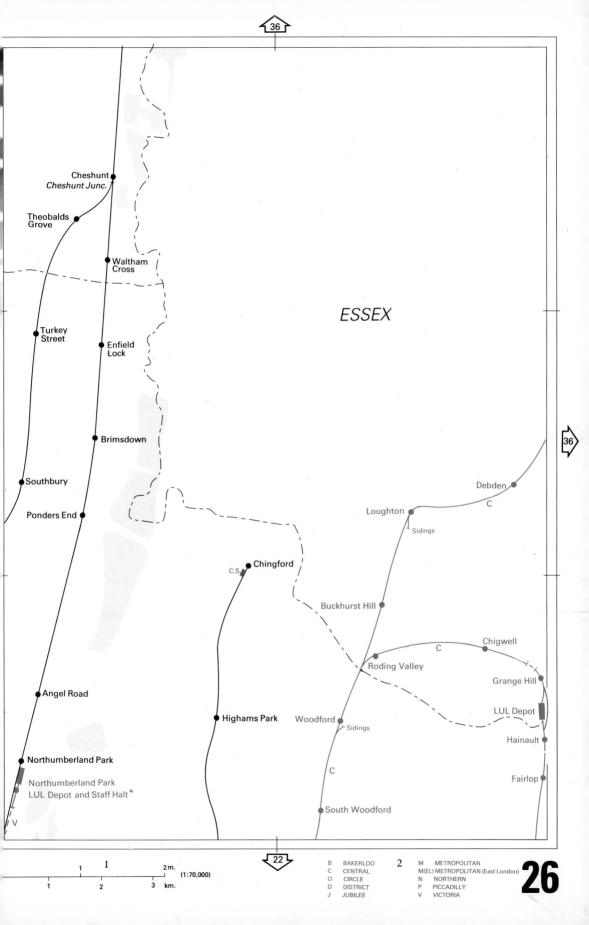

Cheshunt
*Cheshunt Junc.*

Theobalds
Grove

Waltham
Cross

ESSEX

Turkey
Street

Enfield
Lock

Brimsdown

Debden

C

Loughton

Sidings

Southbury

Ponders End

Chingford

C.S.

Buckhurst Hill

Chigwell

C

Roding Valley

Grange Hill

Angel Road

LUL Depot

Highams Park

Woodford

Sidings

Hainault

C

South Woodford

Fairlop

Northumberland Park

Northumberland Park
LUL Depot and Staff Halt*

V

| | | | |
|---|---|---|---|
| B | BAKERLOO | 2 | M | METROPOLITAN |
| C | CENTRAL | | M(EL) | METROPOLITAN (East London) |
| O | CIRCLE | | N | NORTHERN |
| D | DISTRICT | | P | PICCADILLY |
| J | JUBILEE | | V | VICTORIA |

**26**

1    1    2 m.
                 (1:70,000)
1    2    3 km.

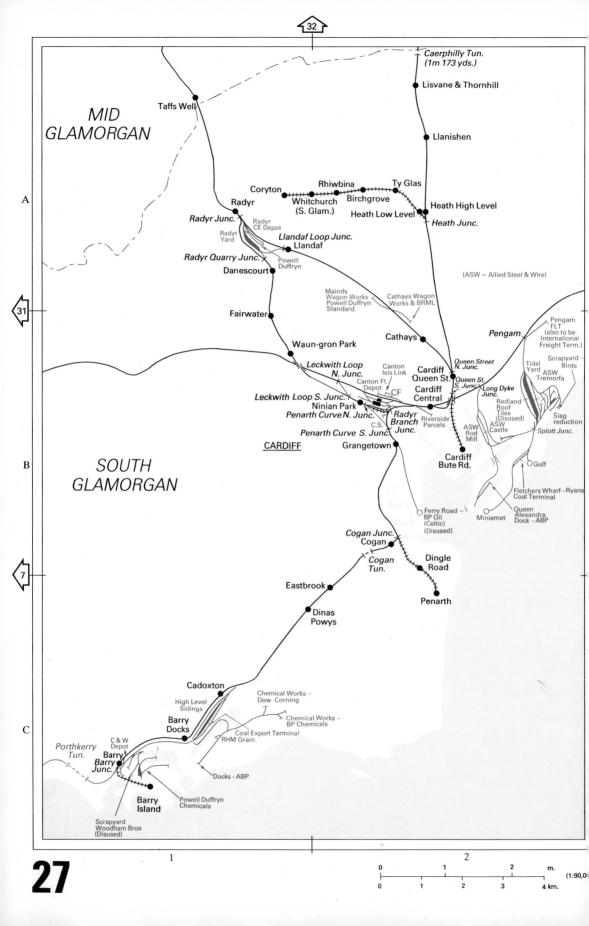

MID
GLAMORGAN

Caerphilly Tun.
(1m 173 yds.)

Lisvane & Thornhill

Taffs Well

Llanishen

A

Coryton          Rhiwbina          Ty Glas
Radyr      Whitchurch    Birchgrove          Heath High Level
(S. Glam.)
*Radyr Junc.*                          Heath Low Level
Radyr          Radyr                          *Heath Junc.*
CE Depot
Radyr
Yard                *Llandaf Loop Junc.*
*Radyr Quarry Junc.*      Llandaf
Powell          (ASW = Allied Steel & Wire)
Duffryn
Danescourt

31

Maindy          Pengam
Wagon Works          FLT
Powell Duffryn          Cathays Wagon          (also to be
Standard          Works & BRML          International
Fairwater                                        Freight Term.)
*Pengam*          Scrapyard
Birds
Waun-gron Park          Cathays          Tidal          ASW
Queen Street          Yard          Tremorfa
*Leckwith Loop*          Canton          N. Junc.
*N. Junc.*          Isis Link          Cardiff          Long Dyke
Canton Ft.          Queen St.      *Queen St.*      *Junc.*          Redland
*Leckwith Loop S. Junc.*      Depot          *S. Junc.*          Roof
CF          Cardiff          Tiles          Slag
Ninian Park          Central      ASW      (Disused)      reduction
*Penarth Curve N. Junc.*          *Radyr*          Rod          ASW
C.S.      *Branch*      Riverside      Mill      Castle      *Splott Junc.*
*Penarth Curve S. Junc.*          *Junc.*      Parcels
CARDIFF          Grangetown          Cardiff
Bute Rd.          Gulf

B          SOUTH          Fletchers Wharf—Ryans
GLAMORGAN          Coal Terminal
Ferry Road—          Queen
BP Oil          Miniemet          Alexandra
(Celtic)          Dock—ABP
(Disused)

*Cogan Junc.*
Cogan

7          *Cogan*          Dingle
*Tun.*          Road
Eastbrook
Penarth
Dinas
Powys

Cadoxton
Chemical Works—
High Level          Dow Corning
Sidings
Barry          Chemical Works—
Docks          BP Chemicals
Coal Export Terminal
C & W          RHM Grain
*Porthkerry*          Depot
*Tun.*          Barry
**Barry**          Docks—ABP
*Junc.*
Barry
Island          Powell Duffryn
Chemicals
Scrapyard
Woodham Bros
(Disused)

C

**27**

1          2

0          1          2          m.
(1:90,0
0          1          2          3          4 km.

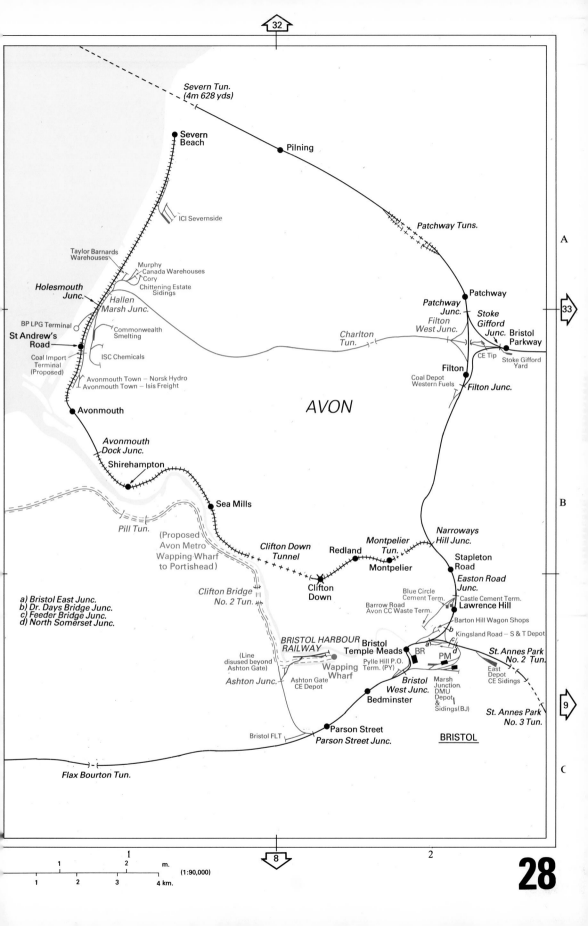

32

Severn Tun.
(4m 628 yds)

Severn
Beach

Pilning

Patchway Tuns.

ICI Severnside

A

Taylor Barnards
Warehouses

Murphy
Canada Warehouses
Cory
Chittening Estate
Sidings

Holesmouth
Junc.

Hallen
Marsh Junc.

Patchway

Patchway
Junc.

Stoke
Gifford
Junc.

Bristol
Parkway

33

BP LPG Terminal

St Andrew's
Road

Commonwealth
Smelting

Coal Import
Terminal
(Proposed)

ISC Chemicals

Filton
West Junc.

Charlton
Tun.

CE Tip

Stoke Gifford
Yard

Avonmouth Town – Norsk Hydro
Avonmouth Town – Isis Freight

Filton

Coal Depot
Western Fuels

Filton Junc.

AVON

Avonmouth

Avonmouth
Dock Junc.

Shirehampton

Sea Mills

Pill Tun.

(Proposed
Avon Metro
Wapping Wharf
to Portishead)

Clifton Down
Tunnel

Redland

Montpelier
Tun.

Montpelier

Narroways
Hill Junc.

Stapleton
Road

B

Clifton Bridge
No. 2 Tun.

Clifton
Down

Easton Road
Junc.

Blue Circle
Cement Term.

Castle Cement Term.

Lawrence Hill

a) Bristol East Junc.
b) Dr. Days Bridge Junc.
c) Feeder Bridge Junc.
d) North Somerset Junc.

Barrow Road
Avon CC Waste Term.

Barton Hill Wagon Shops

Kingsland Road – S & T Depot

BRISTOL HARBOUR
RAILWAY

Bristol
Temple Meads

BR

PM

St. Annes Park
No. 2 Tun.

(Line
disused beyond
Ashton Gate)

Ashton Junc.

Pylle Hill P.O.
Term. (PY)

Ashton Gate
CE Depot

Wapping
Wharf

Bristol
West Junc.

Bedminster

Marsh
Junction
DMU
Depot
& Sidings (BJ)

East
Depot
CE Sidings

St. Annes Park
No. 3 Tun.

9

Bristol FLT

Parson Street
Parson Street Junc.

BRISTOL

C

Flax Bourton Tun.

1

2

m.

1

2

1

2

3

4 km.

(1:90,000)

8

**28**

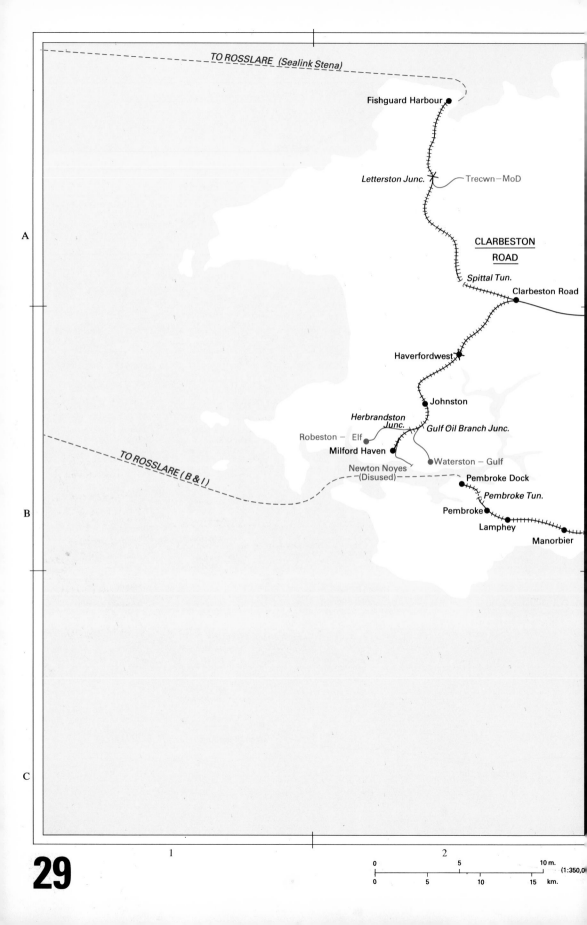

TO ROSSLARE (Sealink Stena)

Fishguard Harbour

*Letterston Junc.* ✕ —— Trecwn—MoD

CLARBESTON
ROAD

*Spittal Tun.*

Clarbeston Road

Haverfordwest

Johnston

*Herbrandston Junc.*

Robeston — Elf

*Gulf Oil Branch Junc.*

Milford Haven

Waterston — Gulf

Newton Noyes
(Disused)

TO ROSSLARE (B & I)

Pembroke Dock

*Pembroke Tun.*

Pembroke

Lamphey

Manorbier

A

B

C

1

2

```
0          5          10 m.
                         (1:350,0
0     5      10    15    km.
```

**29**

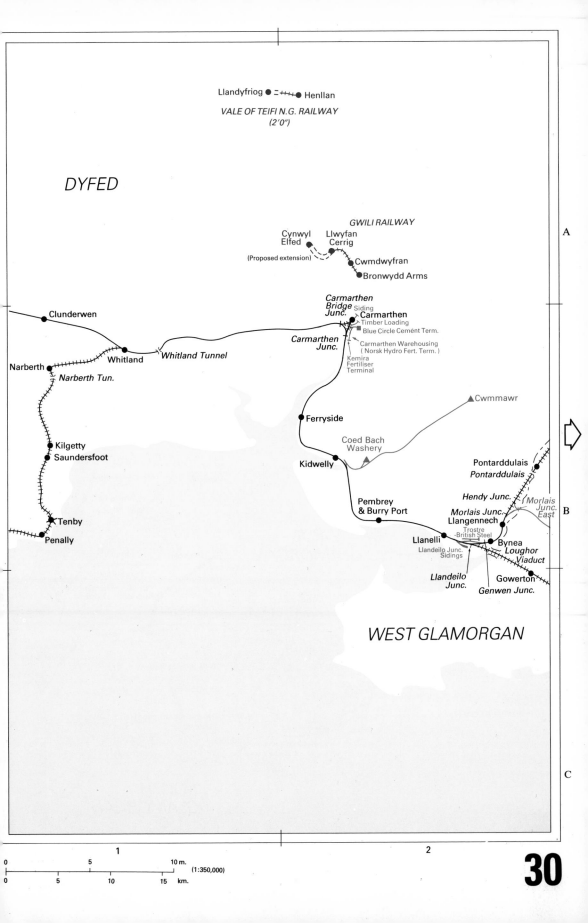

Llandyfriog ● ⚊╫╫╫● Henllan

*VALE OF TEIFI N.G. RAILWAY*
*(2'0")*

DYFED

*GWILI RAILWAY*

Cynwyl
Elfed ●      Llwyfan
              Cerrig ●

(Proposed extension)      ● Cwmdwyfran

              ● Bronwydd Arms

*Carmarthen*
*Bridge* Siding
*Junc.*  ■ Carmarthen
         ■ Timber Loading
         ■ Blue Circle Cement Term.

● Clunderwen

*Carmarthen*
*Junc.*      Carmarthen Warehousing
             ( Norsk Hydro Fert. Term. )

Narberth ●                         Whitland Tunnel
         Whitland ●      Kemira
                          Fertiliser
         *Narberth Tun.*   Terminal

                                              ▲ Cwmmawr

● Ferryside

Coed Bach
Washery
▲

● Kilgetty                    Kidwelly ●                    Pontarddulais ●
● Saundersfoot                                             *Pontarddulais*

                                        Pembrey        *Hendy Junc.*            *Morlais*
                                        & Burry Port ●                          *Junc.*
                                                       *Morlais Junc.*          *East*
▲ Tenby                                                Llangennech ●
● Penally                              Llanelli ●      Trostre
                                       Llandeilo Junc.  -British Steel   ● Bynea
                                       Sidings                           *Loughor*
                                                                         *Viaduct*
                                       *Llandeilo*              ● Gowerton
                                       *Junc.*       *Genwen Junc.*

                                    *WEST GLAMORGAN*

A

B

C

1                                    2

0        5              10 m.
                              (1:350,000)
0      5        10        15    km.

**30**

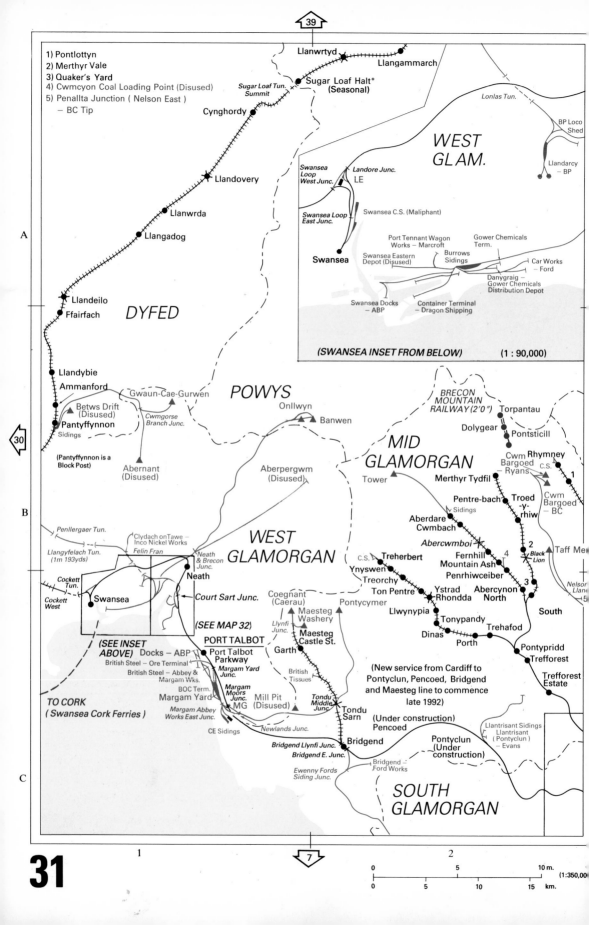

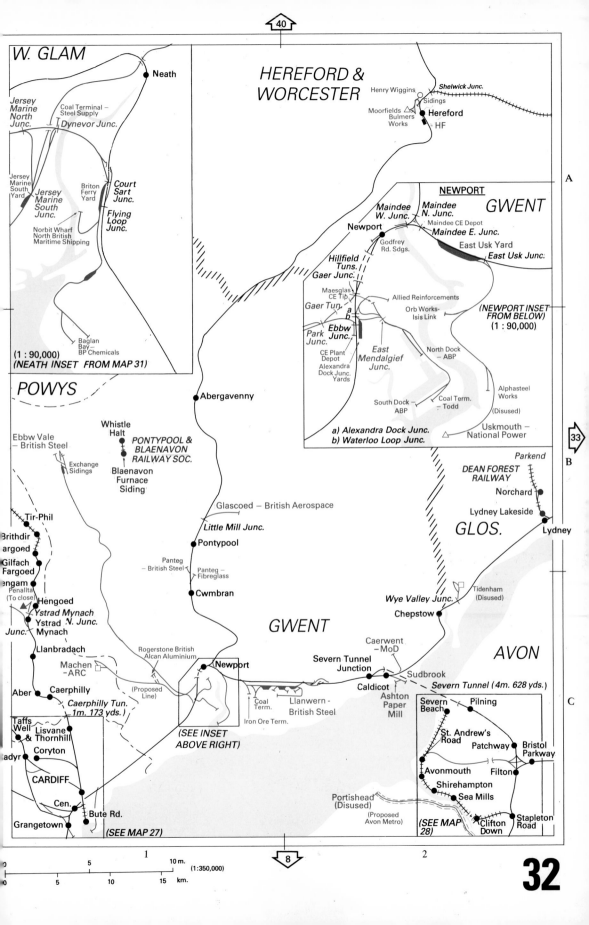

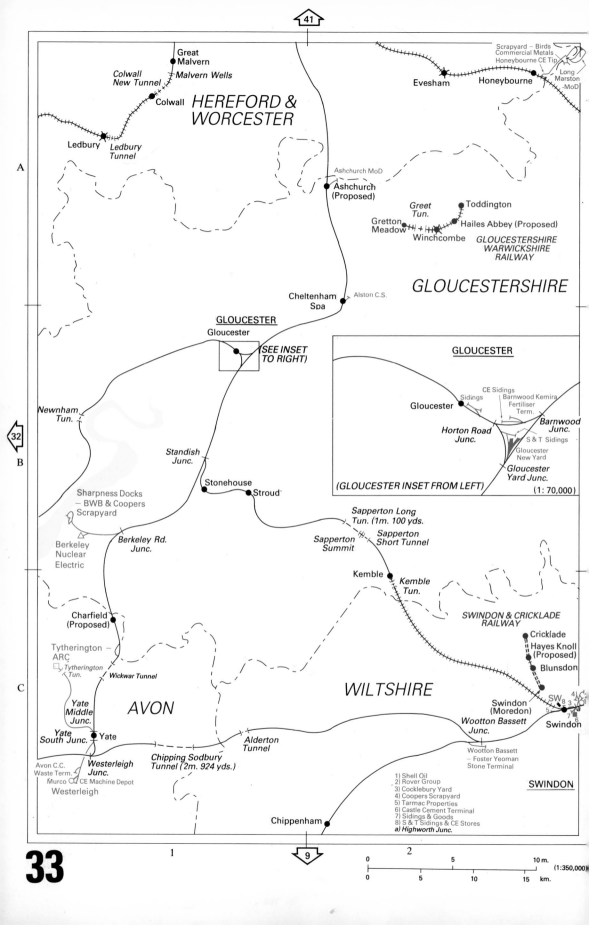

**Great Malvern**

*Colwall New Tunnel*

*Malvern Wells*

**Colwall**

# HEREFORD & WORCESTER

**Evesham**

**Honeybourne**

Scrapyard – Birds
Commercial Metals
Honeybourne CE Tip

Long Marston -MoD

**Ledbury**

*Ledbury Tunnel*

A

Ashchurch MoD

**Ashchurch (Proposed)**

**Toddington**

*Greet Tun.*

*Gretton Meadow*

**Hailes Abbey (Proposed)**

**Winchcombe**

*GLOUCESTERSHIRE WARWICKSHIRE RAILWAY*

# GLOUCESTERSHIRE

**Cheltenham Spa**

Alston C.S.

**GLOUCESTER**

Gloucester

*(SEE INSET TO RIGHT)*

### GLOUCESTER

Gloucester

Sidings

CE Sidings
Barnwood Kemira
Fertiliser Term.

*Barnwood Junc.*

*Horton Road Junc.*

S & T Sidings

Gloucester New Yard

*Gloucester Yard Junc.*

*(GLOUCESTER INSET FROM LEFT)*

*(1: 70,000)*

*Newnham Tun.*

B

*Standish Junc.*

**Stonehouse**

**Stroud**

*Sapperton Long Tun. (1m. 100 yds.*

*Sapperton Short Tunnel*

*Sapperton Summit*

Sharpness Docks
– BWB & Coopers
Scrapyard

*Berkeley Rd. Junc.*

Berkeley Nuclear Electric

**Kemble**

*Kemble Tun.*

*SWINDON & CRICKLADE RAILWAY*

**Cricklade**

**Hayes Knoll (Proposed)**

**Blunsdon**

**Charfield (Proposed)**

Tytherington – ARC

*Tytherington Tun.*

*Wickwar Tunnel*

# WILTSHIRE

**Swindon (Moredon)**

SW 4
8 3
5 a

**Swindon**

C

*Yate Middle Junc.*

# AVON

*Yate South Junc.* **Yate**

*Alderton Tunnel*

*Wootton Bassett Junc.*

Avon C.C. Waste Term.

*Westerleigh Junc.*

Murco CE Machine Depot

Westerleigh

*Chipping Sodbury Tunnel (2m. 924 yds.)*

Wootton Bassett – Foster Yeoman Stone Terminal

1) Shell Oil
2) Rover Group
3) Cocklebury Yard
4) Coopers Scrapyard
5) Tarmac Properties
6) Castle Cement Terminal
7) Sidings & Goods
8) S & T Sidings & CE Stores
*a) Highworth Junc.*

# SWINDON

**Chippenham**

1

2

0     5     10 m.

(1:350,000)

0   5   10   15 km.

WARWICKSHIRE

NORTHAMPTONSHIRE

BUCKS

Foster-Yeoman and
Redland Stone Terminals

Banbury Yard

*Campden
Tun.*

Banbury
BP

Sidings

Kings Sutton

OXFORDSHIRE

*Aynho Junc.*

Aynho Park Junc.
*Ardley Tunnel*

A

Moreton-
in-Marsh

Heyford

Kingham

Bicester North
Bicester Town

Tackley

Shipton

Charlbury

Ascott-under
Wychwood

Finstock

*BICESTER
MIL. RLY.*

Arncott

*Brill
Tun.*

Combe

Handborough

Islip
Banbury Road
ARC Stone Term.
*Wolvercot Junc.*

*Wolvercote Tun.*

Appleford

*Oxford North Junc.*

**OXFORD**

ARC Stone Term.
& Waste Term.

OX

C.S.

Oxford

B

Rover Group

Didcot Distribution Centre
( Milton ) – Lansdown
International Facilities
& Nedlloyd

Didcot –
National Power

*Didcot
North
Junc.*

Hinksey
Yard

**Morris Cowley**

*Kennington
Junc.*

MAT Car Terminal

Freight Depot
United Bennetts Freight Term.

*Didcot West
Curve Junc.*

CE Tip

Great
Western
Society

Littlemore –
BP Oil
( Hartwells )

Radley

*Foxhall Junc.*
Steventon Bulk Haulage

Didcot
Yard

Culham

**(DIDCOT INSET
FROM RIGHT)**

*Didcot West Junc.*
Didcot Parkway

*Didcot East Junc.*

(1: 70,000)

Appleford
*(SEE INSET
TO LEFT)*

Wallingford

Didcot
Parkway

*CHOLSEY &
WALLINGFORD
RAILWAY*

Cholsey

Goring &
Streatley

C

BERKSHIRE

Pangbourne

Tilehurst

0     5     10 m.
(1:350,000)

0   5   10   15   km.

**34**

**BEDFORDSHIRE**

Fenny Stratford
Flyover Junc.
Denbigh Hall
South Junc.
BRML (ZN)
Wolverton
Transport &
Warehousing
Facilities Ltd.
CE & OLE
Depot
BY
ARC Stone
Terminal
C.S.
S & T Sidings
P.O. Term.
Bletchley
Bletchley
Junc.
Stone Term.
-Peakstone
Flyover Junc.
(1 : 90,000)
(BLETCHLEY INSET FROM RIGHT)

**BLETCHLEY**

Milton
Keynes
Central
Bletchley
Fenny
Stratford
(SEE INSET TO LEFT)

Kempston
Hardwick
Forders Sidings
Shanks & McEwan Landfill
Stewartby
Millbrook
CE Tip
Lidlington
Woburn
Sands
Ridgmont
Aspley Guise
Ampthill
Tuns.

Elstow – Redland
Stone Terminal

Biggleswade
Plasmor
Brick
Terminal

Arlesey

Flitwick

Harlington

Cambridge
Junc.
CE Plant Depot
Hitchin
CE
Yard

A

Winslow*

Claydon L.N.E. Junc.
Calvert – Shanks &
McEwan Waste Terminal

Linslade Tuns.
Leighton
Buzzard

LEIGHTON BUZZARD
RLY. (2'0")

Dunstable
(Disused)

Leagrave
Sidings
Limbury Rd.
Tarmac Stone Term.
Foster Yeoman Stone Term.
Luton
Luton
Bute St

Harpenden

Grendon Underwood Junc.

Quainton Road*

Akeman Street –
Firmin Coates

Cheddington

GREAT WHIPSNADE RLY.
(2'6")

Goods & Hartwells
Aylesbury
C.S.
Aylesbury Diesel Depot
(AL)

Tring

Tring
Summit

**HERTFORDSHIRE**

34

Haddenham &
Thame Parkway

Stoke
Mandeville

Wendover

Northchurch
Tuns.

Berkhamsted

St. Albans
Abbey
St. Albans

Thame
(Disused)

Little
Kimble

Monks
Risborough

Hemel
Hempstead
Apsley
Park St.

Post Office Term.

(SEE MAP
24)

B

(Chinnor & Princes
Risborough Railway
Association
planning
to preserve
this line)

Princes
Risborough

Saunderton
Summit

Chinnor
(Disused)

Saunderton

Dutchlands
Summit

Great
Missenden

Chesham

M

(MANTLES WOOD)

BR
LUL

Chalfont
& Latimer

Amersham

King's
Langley

Radlett

Watford

Croxley
Green

Watford Junc.

Stanmore

Edgware

**BUCKINGHAMSHIRE**

Chorley
Wood

Rickmansworth

M

Moor
Park

J

N

(READING INSET FROM BELOW)

Reading
Yards
CE
Sidings
S & T Sidings
Reading
Reading
New Junc.
Reading
West
Junc.
RG
Westbury
Line Junc.
C.S.
Reading
Spur Junc.
Reading
West
Oxford Road Junc.

**READING**

Southcote
Junc.
(1 : 90,000)

High Wycombe

Beaconsfield
Seer Green

Whitehouse
Tun.

(SEE MAP 23)

Denham

Harrow-on-
the-Hill

M/P
Rayners
Lane

(SEE MA

Gerrards
Cross
Denham Golf
Club

West
Ruislip

C

**GREATER
LONDON**

Uxbridge

Marlow
Bourne End

Cookham

Redland
Stone Term.

**SLOUGH**

Furze Platt

Henley-on-Thames
Shiplake

**OXON.**
**BERKSHIRE**

Taplow
Burnham
Shell
Slough

Maidenhead

Langley
Total

Langley
Iver

West
Drayton

Ealing
Bdy.

Wargrave

Windsor & Eton
Central
Windsor & Eton Riverside
Sunnymeads

Datchet

Heathrow

P

(SEE INSET
ABOVE)

Reading

Twyford

Wraysbury

(SEE MAP 19)

Feltham

Richmond

Reading West

1

DL  DOCKLANDS
B   BAKERLOO
C   CENTRAL
O   CIRCLE
D   DISTRICT
J   JUBILEE

M    METROPOLITAN
M(EL) METROPOLITAN (East London)
N    NORTHERN
P    PICCADILLY
V    VICTORIA

35

11

2

15

16

0       5
0       5       10      15   km.

10 m.
(1:350,000)

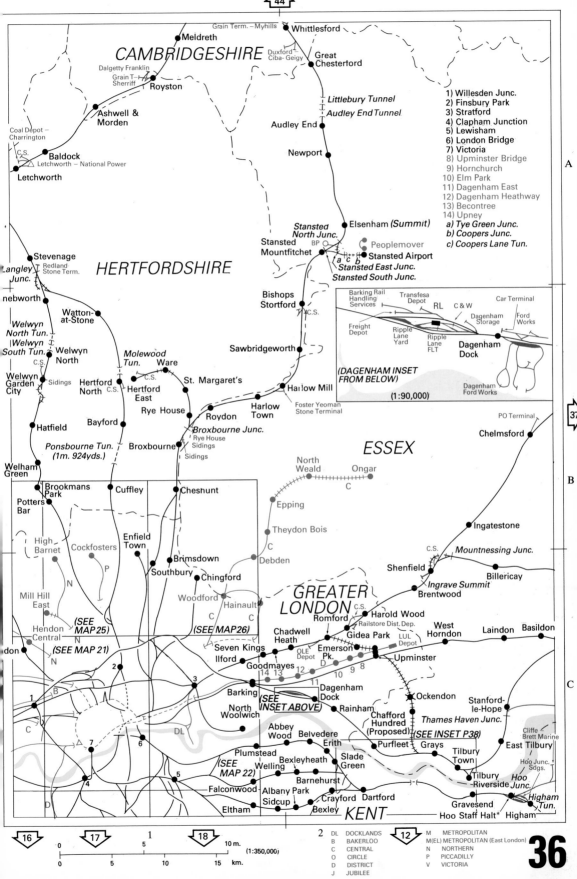

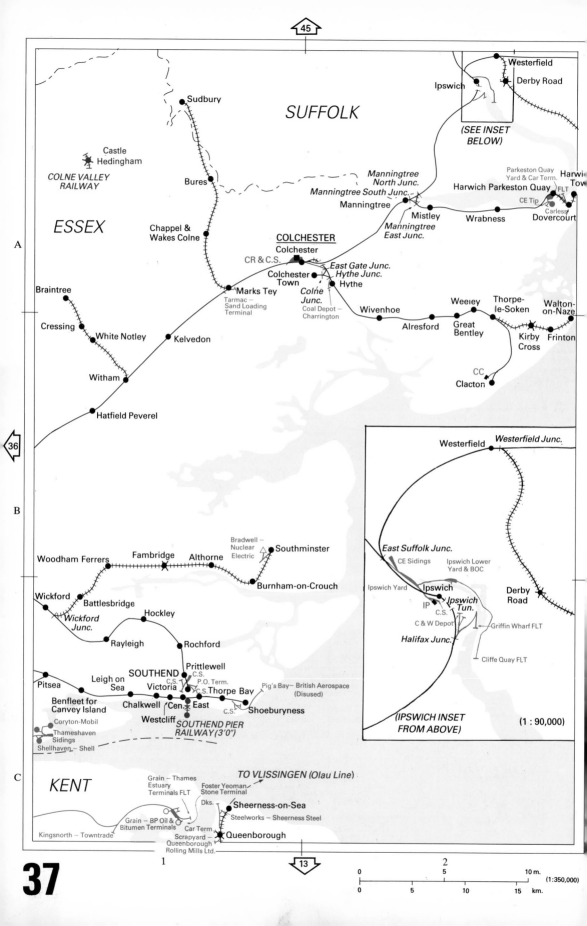

SUFFOLK

Westerfield
Ipswich
Derby Road
(SEE INSET BELOW)

Sudbury

Castle
Hedingham
COLNE VALLEY
RAILWAY

ESSEX

Bures

Manningtree North Junc.
Manningtree South Junc.
Manningtree
Mistley
Wrabness
Parkeston Quay Yard & Car Term.
Harwich Parkeston Quay
FLT
Harwich Town
CE Tip
Carless
Dovercourt

Chappel &
Wakes Colne

Manningtree East Junc.

COLCHESTER
Colchester
CR & C.S.
Colchester Town
East Gate Junc.
Hythe Junc.
Hythe
Colne Junc.
Coal Depot – Charrington

A

Marks Tey
Tarmac – Sand Loading Terminal

Braintree

Weeley
Thorpe-le-Soken
Walton-on-Naze

Cressing

White Notley

Kelvedon

Wivenhoe
Alresford
Great Bentley
Kirby Cross
Frinton

Witham

Hatfield Peverel

CC
Clacton

Westerfield
Westerfield Junc.

B

East Suffolk Junc.
CE Sidings
Ipswich Lower Yard & BOC
Ipswich Yard
Ipswich
IP
C.S.
Ipswich Tun.
C & W Depot
Derby Road
Griffin Wharf FLT

Halifax Junc.
Cliffe Quay FLT

Bradwell – Nuclear Electric
Southminster

Woodham Ferrers
Fambridge
Althorne

Burnham-on-Crouch

Wickford
Battlesbridge
Wickford Junc.

Hockley

Rayleigh
Rochford

Pitsea

SOUTHEND
Prittlewell
C.S.
P.O. Term.
Leigh on Sea
Victoria
C.S.
Thorpe Bay
Pig's Bay – British Aerospace (Disused)

Benfleet for Canvey Island
Chalkwell
Cen.
East
C.S.
Shoeburyness

Coryton-Mobil
Thameshaven Sidings
Shellhaven – Shell

Westcliff
SOUTHEND PIER RAILWAY (3'0")

(IPSWICH INSET FROM ABOVE)
(1 : 90,000)

C

KENT

Grain – Thames Estuary Terminals FLT
Foster Yeoman Stone Terminal

TO VLISSINGEN (Olau Line)

Dks.
Sheerness-on-Sea
Steelworks – Sheerness Steel

Grain – BP Oil & Bitumen Terminals
Kingsnorth – Towntrade
Car Term.
Scrapyard – Queenborough Rolling Mills Ltd.
Queenborough

1

2
5
10 m.
(1:350,000)
0    5    10    15    km.

Talybont

Llanaber

Barmouth

*Barmouth Viaduct*

Porth Penrhyn

Morfa Mawddach

**GWYNEDD**

*FAIRBOURNE RAILWAY (1'0¼")*

Fairbourne

Fairbourne

Llwyngwril

*TALYLLYN RAILWAY (2'3")*

Llangelynin (Temp. closed)

Abergynolwyn

*Quarry Siding*

Nant Gwernol

Dolgoch Falls

Tonfanau

**MACHYNLLETH RADIO SIGNALLING CENTRE**

A

Tywyn Wharf

Brynglas

Rhydyronen

Sidings

Tywyn

Machynlleth

Tywyn Pendre

MN

**POWYS**

*Aberdovey Tuns.*

39

*No. 2* *No.1*

*No.4*

Dovey Junction

Aberdovey

*No. 3*

Penhelig

Borth

**DYFED**

Felixstowe:

North FLT

Trimley

*Felixstowe Beach Junc.*

Felixstowe

Docks – Felixstowe Dock & Railway Co.

Felixstowe Docks

South FLT

**FELIXSTOWE** – **ZEEBRUGGE** (P&O)
     – **HARWICH**
       (Orwell & Harwich Nav. Co.)
     – **HOEK VAN HOLLAND** (Sealink)

**PARKESTON QUAY** – **ESJBERG** (*Scandinavian Seaways*)
     – **GOTEBORG** (*Scandinavian Seaways*)
     – **HAMBURG** (*Scandinavian Seaways*)
     – **KRISTIANSAND/OSLO** (*Fred Olsen*)

Shell

Aberystwyth

Glanrafon

Llanbadarn

Capel Bangor

Aberffrwd

Rheidol Falls

B

Nantyronen

Rhiwfron

Devil's Bridge

*VALE OF RHEIDOL RAILWAY (1'11½")*

Powell Duffryn Oils

**ESSEX**

(Tilbury Riverside is proposed for closure)

Gulf

**Purfleet**

Lafarge Aluminious Cement Works (Disused)

*West Thurrock Junc.*

Unitank

Grays

Esso

Van den Berghs

Tilbury FLT

Slade Green

*Slade Green Junc.*

Purfleet Thames Terminal (Otis Euro Transrail)

Foster Yeoman Stone Terminal

Thames Matex

West Thurrock – Proctor & Gamble

Tilbury Grain Terminal

**Tilbury Town**

*Tilbury E. Junc.*

36

C.S.

*Tilbury W. Junc.*

rry Street

rk Junc.

*Crayford Creek Junc.*

*Crayford Spur 'A' Junc.*

Dartford

C.S.

Tilbury Northfleet Hope FLT

*Tilbury South Junc.*

Tilbury Riverside

Gravesend West St.

*(White Horse Ferries)*

*Crayford Spur 'B'*

*Dartford Junc.*

**DARTFORD**

*Greenhithe Tun.*

Stone Crossing

Greenhithe

Swanscombe

C

Northfleet

Northfleet – Blue Circle Cement Works

Gravesend

(*INSET FROM MAP 36*) (1:90,000)

**KENT**

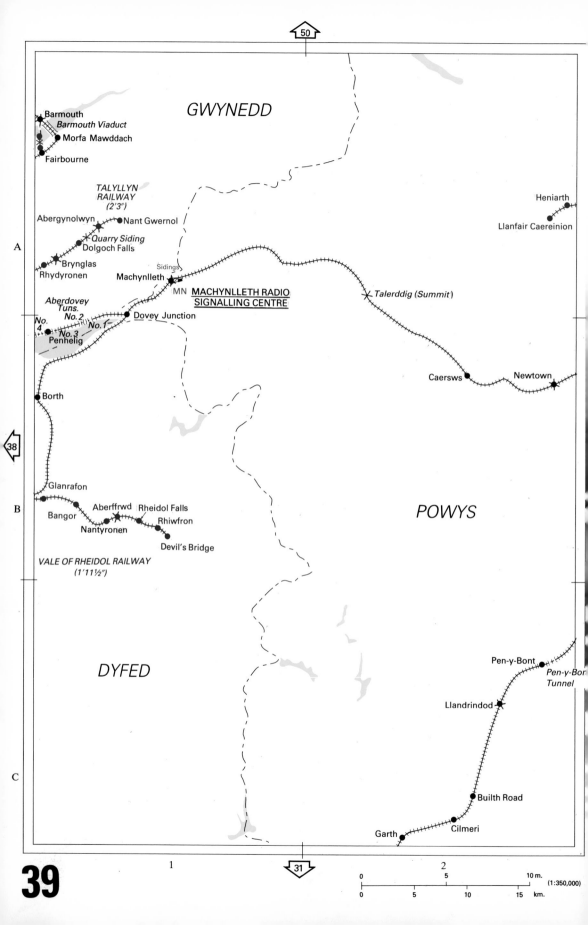

50

GWYNEDD

Barmouth
*Barmouth Viaduct*
Morfa Mawddach
Fairbourne

Heniarth

*TALYLLYN
RAILWAY
(2'3")*

Llanfair Caereinion

Abergynolwyn — Nant Gwernol

*Quarry Siding*
Dolgoch Falls

A

Brynglas
Rhydyronen

Sidings

Machynlleth

MN **MACHYNLLETH RADIO
SIGNALLING CENTRE**

Talerddig (Summit)

*Aberdovey
Tuns.
No. 2*

No.
4

*No. 1*

Dovey Junction

*No. 3*
Penhelig

Caersws

Newtown

38

Borth

Glanrafon

B

Bangor

Aberffrwd
Nantyronen

Rheidol Falls

Rhiwfron

Devil's Bridge

POWYS

*VALE OF RHEIDOL RAILWAY
(1'11½")*

Pen-y-Bont

*Pen-y-Bont
Tunnel*

DYFED

Llandrindod

C

Builth Road

Garth

Cilmeri

1

31

2

0          5          10 m.

(1:350,000)

0     5     10     15   km.

**39**

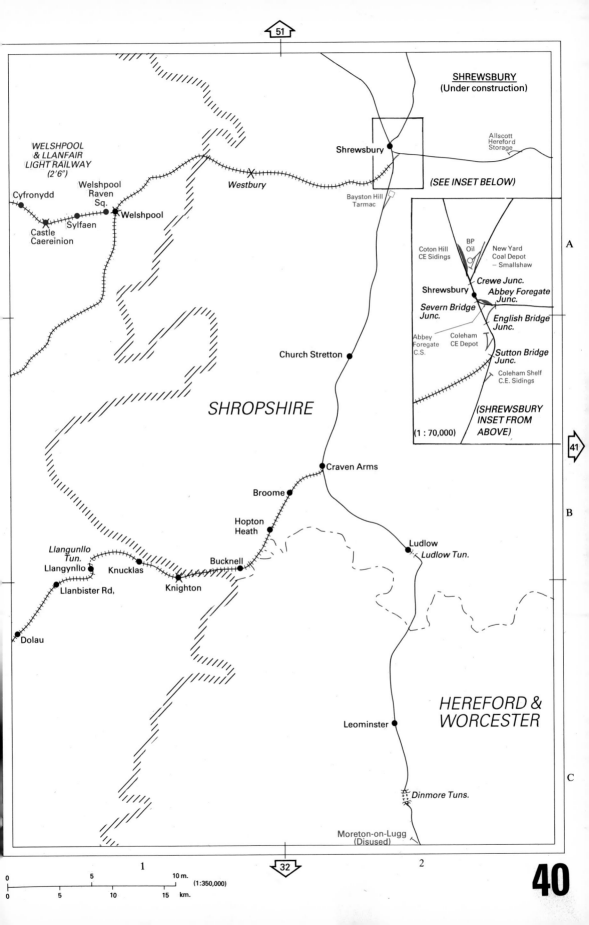

51

SHREWSBURY
(Under construction)

WELSHPOOL
& LLANFAIR
LIGHT RAILWAY
(2'6")

Cyfronydd

Welshpool
Raven
Sq.

Welshpool

Sylfaen

Castle
Caereinion

Westbury

Shrewsbury

Allscott
Hereford
Storage

Bayston Hill
Tarmac

(SEE INSET BELOW)

A

Coton Hill
CE Sidings

BP
Oil

New Yard
Coal Depot
– Smallshaw

Shrewsbury

Crewe Junc.

Abbey Foregate
Junc.

Severn Bridge
Junc.

English Bridge
Junc.

Abbey
Foregate
C.S.

Coleham
CE Depot

Sutton Bridge
Junc.

Coleham Shelf
C.E. Sidings

(SHREWSBURY
INSET FROM
ABOVE)

(1 : 70,000)

41

Church Stretton

SHROPSHIRE

B

Craven Arms

Broome

Hopton
Heath

Ludlow

Ludlow Tun.

Llangunllo
Tun.

Llangynllo

Knucklas

Bucknell

Llanbister Rd.

Knighton

Dolau

HEREFORD &
WORCESTER

Leominster

C

Dinmore Tuns.

Moreton-on-Lugg
(Disused)

1

10 m.

2

0     5     10 m.

(1:350,000)

0     5     10     15     km.

32

**40**

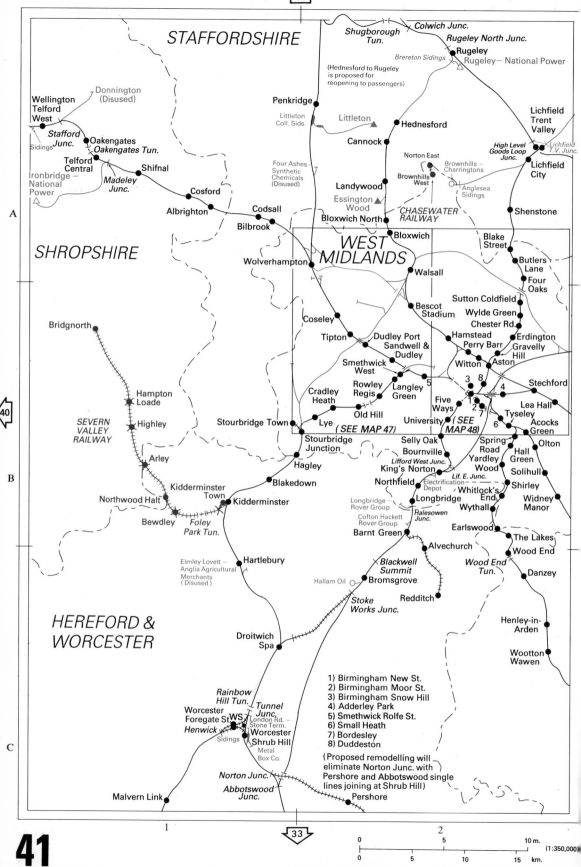

STAFFORDSHIRE

*Shugborough Tun.*

*Colwich Junc.*

*Rugeley North Junc.*

*Brereton Sidings*

Rugeley
Rugeley — National Power

(Hednesford to Rugeley is proposed for reopening to passengers)

Penkridge

Littleton Coll. Sids.

Littleton

Hednesford

Cannock

Lichfield Trent Valley

*High Level Goods Loop Junc.*

*Lichfield T.V. Junc.*

Wellington Telford West

Donnington (Disused)

*Stafford Junc.*

Sidings

Oakengates
*Oakengates Tun.*

Telford Central

*Madeley Junc.*

Shifnal

Cosford

Albrighton

Codsall

Bilbrook

Ironbridge — National Power

SHROPSHIRE

Four Ashes - Synthetic Chemicals (Disused)

Landywood

*Essington Wood*

Bloxwich North

Norton East

Brownhills Charringtons

Brownhills West

Anglesea Sidings

*CHASEWATER RAILWAY*

Lichfield City

Shenstone

Wolverhampton

Bloxwich

WEST MIDLANDS

Walsall

Bescot Stadium

Blake Street

Butlers Lane

Four Oaks

Sutton Coldfield

Wylde Green

Chester Rd.

Bridgnorth

Coseley

Tipton

Dudley Port

Sandwell & Dudley

Smethwick West

Hamstead
Perry Barr

Witton

Erdington

Gravelly Hill

Aston

Stechford

Hampton Loade

*SEVERN VALLEY RAILWAY*

Highley

Cradley Heath

Rowley Regis

Langley Green

5

3  8

1

2  7

4

Lea Hall

Tyseley

Acocks Green

Olton

Five Ways

*(SEE MAP 48)*

6

Old Hill

University

Lye

*( SEE MAP 47)*

Stourbridge Town

Selly Oak

Bournville

Spring Road

Hall Green

Arley

Stourbridge Junction

*Lifford West Junc.*

Yardley Wood

Solihull

Hagley

King's Norton

*Lif. E. Junc.*

Shirley

Kidderminster Town

Blakedown

Northfield

Electrification Depot

*Whitlock's End*

Widney Manor

Northwood Halt

Bewdley

*Foley Park Tun.*

Kidderminster

Longbridge — Rover Group

Longbridge

Wythall

*Halesowen Junc.*

Cofton Hackett Rover Group

Earlswood

The Lakes

Wood End

Hartlebury

Barnt Green

Alvechurch

*Wood End Tun.*

Danzey

Elmley Lovett - Anglia Agricultural Merchants ( Disused )

*Blackwell Summit*

Bromsgrove

Hallam Oil

Redditch

Henley-in-Arden

HEREFORD & WORCESTER

Droitwich Spa

*Stoke Works Junc.*

Wootton Wawen

*Rainbow Hill Tun.*

*Tunnel Junc.*

Worcester Foregate St.

WS

London Rd. - Stone Term.

*Henwick*

Worcester Shrub Hill

Sidings

Metal Box Co.

1) Birmingham New St.
2) Birmingham Moor St.
3) Birmingham Snow Hill
4) Adderley Park
5) Smethwick Rolfe St.
6) Small Heath
7) Bordesley
8) Duddeston

(Proposed remodelling will eliminate Norton Junc. with Pershore and Abbotswood single lines joining at Shrub Hill)

Malvern Link

*Norton Junc.*

*Abbotswood Junc.*

Pershore

0        5        10 m.

(1:350,000)

0    5    10    15 km.

**41**

A

40

B

C

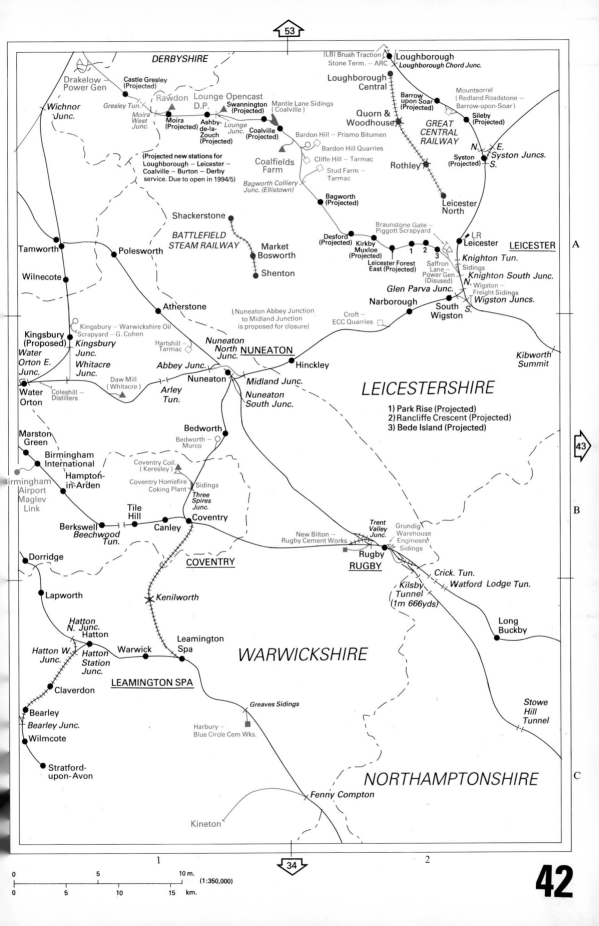

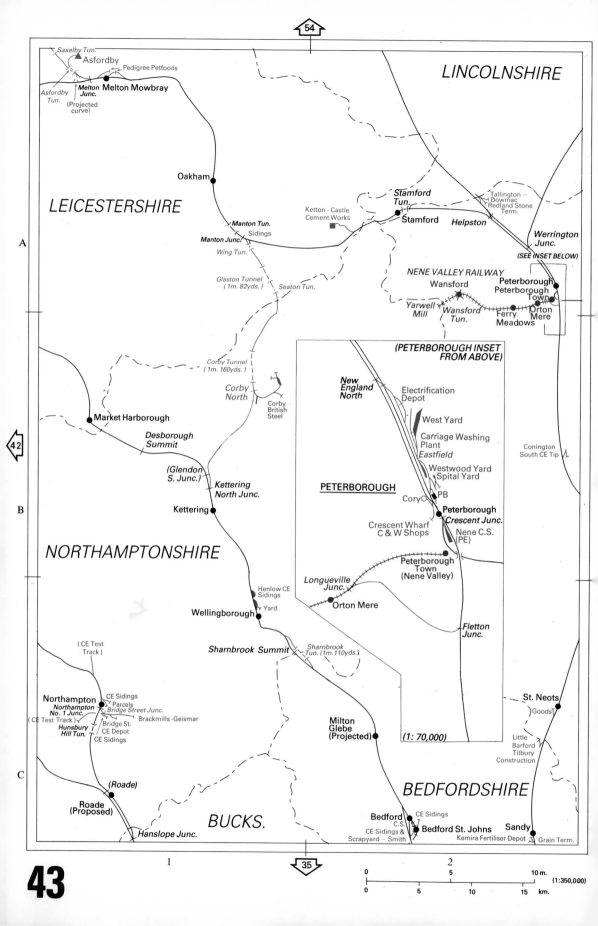

LINCOLNSHIRE

Saxelby Tun.
▲ Asfordby
Pedigree Petfoods

Asfordby Tun.
Melton Junc. Melton Mowbray

(Projected curve)

LEICESTERSHIRE

Oakham

Stamford Tun.
Stamford
Helpston

Ketton - Castle Cement Works

Tallington –
Dowmac
Redland Stone Term.

Manton Tun.
Sidings
Manton Junc.

Wing Tun.

Werrington Junc.

(SEE INSET BELOW)

A

Glaston Tunnel
(1m. 82yds.)
Seaton Tun.

NENE VALLEY RAILWAY

Wansford

Peterborough
Peterborough
Town

Yarwell Mill
Wansford Tun.
Ferry Meadows
Orton Mere

(PETERBOROUGH INSET FROM ABOVE)

Corby Tunnel
(1m. 160yds.)

New England North
Electrification Depot
West Yard

Corby North

Corby British Steel

Carriage Washing Plant
Eastfield

Conington South CE Tip

Market Harborough

Desborough Summit

Westwood Yard
Spital Yard

PETERBOROUGH

(Glendon S. Junc.)

Kettering North Junc.

Cory
PB

Peterborough
Crescent Junc.

42

B

Kettering

Crescent Wharf
C & W Shops

Nene C.S. (PE)

NORTHAMPTONSHIRE

Longueville Junc.

Peterborough Town (Nene Valley)

Henlow CE Sidings
Yard

Orton Mere

Wellingborough

Fletton Junc.

Sharnbrook Summit
Sharnbrook Tun. (1m.110yds.)

(CE Test Track)

St. Neots
Goods

Northampton
Northampton No. 1 Junc.
(CE Test Track)
Hunsbury Hill Tun.

CE Sidings
Parcels
Bridge Street Junc.

Brackmills -Geismar

Bridge St.
CE Depot
CE Sidings

Milton Glebe (Projected)

(1: 70,000)

Little Barford Tilbury Construction

C

(Roade)

Roade (Proposed)

Hanslope Junc.

BUCKS.

Bedford
C.S.
CE Sidings & Scrapyard – Smith

CE Sidings
Bedford St. Johns

Kemira Fertiliser Depot

BEDFORDSHIRE

Sandy

Grain Term.

1

2

0      5      10 m.
(1:350,000)
0      5      10      15   km.

Bentinck & Alexandra Docks – ABP
Dow Chemicals Works
**Kings Lynn**
Kings Lynn Harbour – Dalgetty Franklin
Sidings & Goods
Campbells Soups
South Lynn British Sugar
*Harbour Junc.*
South Lynn Grain – Banks
Middleton Towers - British Industrial Sand

**Watlington**

**NORFOLK**

A

**Wisbech***
Spillers Freight Terminal
Metal Box Co. (Disused)

**Downham Market**

Whitemoor Yard (Disused)
MR
*Whitemoor Junc.*
**March**
*March East Junc.*
**Whittlesea**
Anglia Industrial Merchants
*March West Junc.*
Marcroft Wagon Repair Sidings

**Manea**

**Littleport**

**-Lakenheath**

*Ely West Junc.*
**Shippea Hill**

45

**CAMBRIDGESHIRE**

Distribution Depot – Papworth (Potter Group)

B

Sidings
*Ely North Junc.*
**Ely**
*Ely Dock Junc.*

**SUFFOLK**

**Huntingdon**

Fen Drayton – ARC Sand

Offord Freight Terminal – Superior International (Disused)

*Soham*

Snailwell – Firmin Coates (Disused)
Snailwell – Scrapyard Mayer Newman
**Kennett**
Kennett Redland Aggr.

**Waterbeach**
Chesterton CE Depot & Foster Yeoman Stone Terminal

*Chippenham Junc.*
*Warren Hill Tunnel*
Grain Term. – Dower. – Wood

**Cambridge Parkway (Projected)**

**Newmarket**

*Chesterton Junc.*
Barnwell – BP
*Coldham Lane Junc.*
Coldham Lane - Esso
CA
**Cambridge**
Brooklands Avenue – Charrington Oil
Coalfields Goods
Yard & C.S.

**Dullingham**

C

**CAMBRIDGE**

*Shepreth Branch Junc.*
**Shelford**

Barrington Rugby Cem. Wks.
**Shepreth**
**Foxton**

1

5        10 m.
(1:350,000)
5      10      15   km.

2

**44**

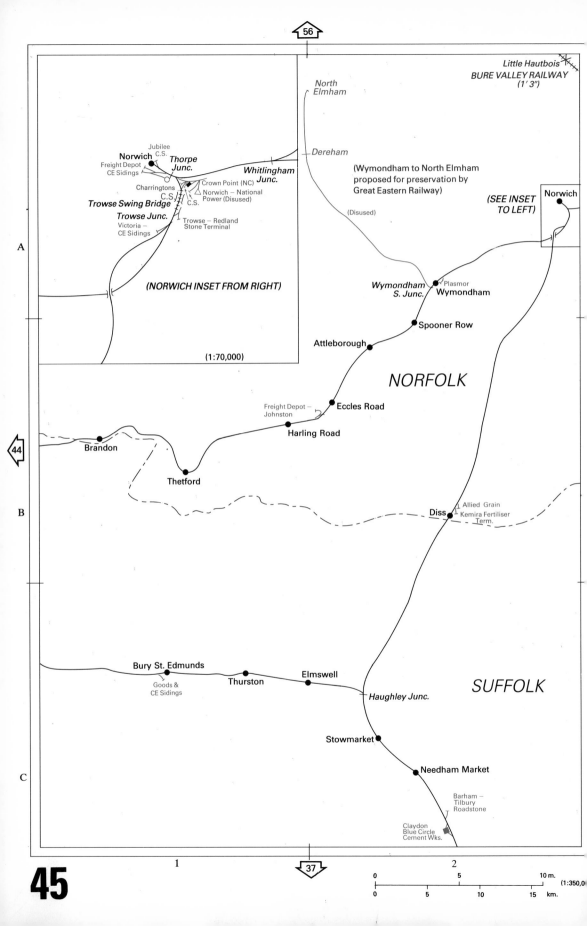

56

*Little Hautbois*
**BURE VALLEY RAILWAY**
*(1' 3")*

North
Elmham

Dereham

(Wymondham to North Elmham
proposed for preservation by
Great Eastern Railway)

(Disused)

*(SEE INSET
TO LEFT)*

Norwich

**Norwich INSET (from top-left inset)**

Jubilee
C.S.
**Norwich**  *Thorpe*
*Junc.*
Freight Depot –
CE Sidings
Charringtons
C.S.
*Trowse Swing Bridge*  C.S.
*Trowse Junc.*
Victoria –
CE Sidings

*Whitlingham
Junc.*

Crown Point (NC)
Norwich – National
Power (Disused)

Trowse – Redland
Stone Terminal

*(NORWICH INSET FROM RIGHT)*

(1:70,000)

*Wymondham
S. Junc.*  Plasmor
**Wymondham**

*NORFOLK*

**Spooner Row**

**Attleborough**

**Eccles Road**

Freight Depot –
Johnston

**Harling Road**

44

**Brandon**

**Thetford**

Diss  Allied Grain
Kemira Fertiliser
Term.

**Bury St. Edmunds**
Goods &
CE Sidings
**Thurston**  **Elmswell**

*SUFFOLK*

*Haughley Junc.*

**Stowmarket**

**Needham Market**

Barham –
Tilbury
Roadstone

Claydon
Blue Circle
Cement Wks.

**45**

1

37

2

0       5       10 m.
                   (1:350,0
0   5   10   15   km.

A

B

C

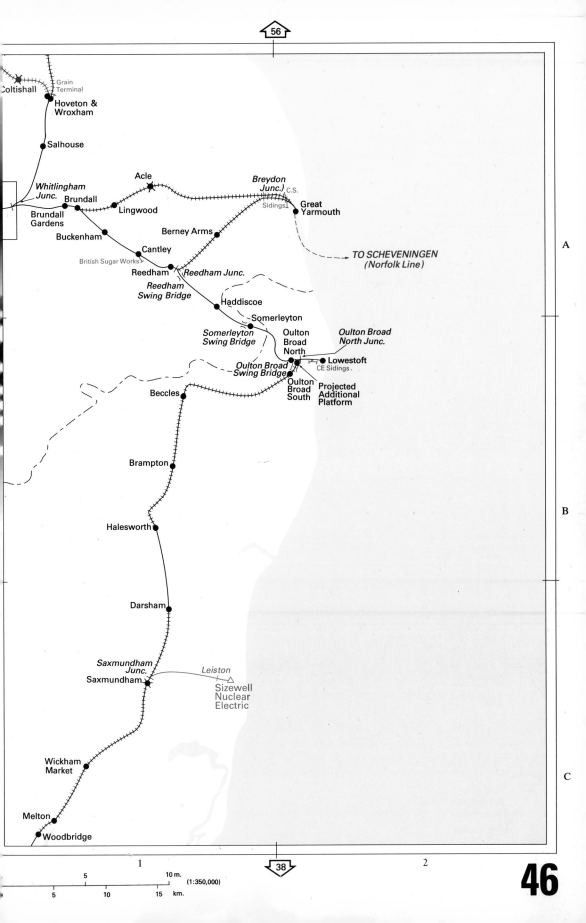

Coltishall

Grain Terminal

Hoveton & Wroxham

Salhouse

Acle

*Whitlingham Junc.*

Brundall

Lingwood

Brundall Gardens

Buckenham

Berney Arms

*Breydon Junc.* C.S.

Sidings

Great Yarmouth

Cantley

British Sugar Works

Reedham

*Reedham Junc.*

*Reedham Swing Bridge*

Haddiscoe

**TO SCHEVENINGEN**
(Norfolk Line)

Somerleyton

*Somerleyton Swing Bridge*

Oulton Broad North

*Oulton Broad North Junc.*

*Oulton Broad Swing Bridge*

Lowestoft

CE Sidings

Oulton Broad South

Projected Additional Platform

Beccles

Brampton

Halesworth

Darsham

*Saxmundham Junc.*

Saxmundham

Leiston

Sizewell Nuclear Electric

Wickham Market

Melton

Woodbridge

A

B

C

1

2

5       10 m.

(1:350,000)

5       10       15 km.

**46**

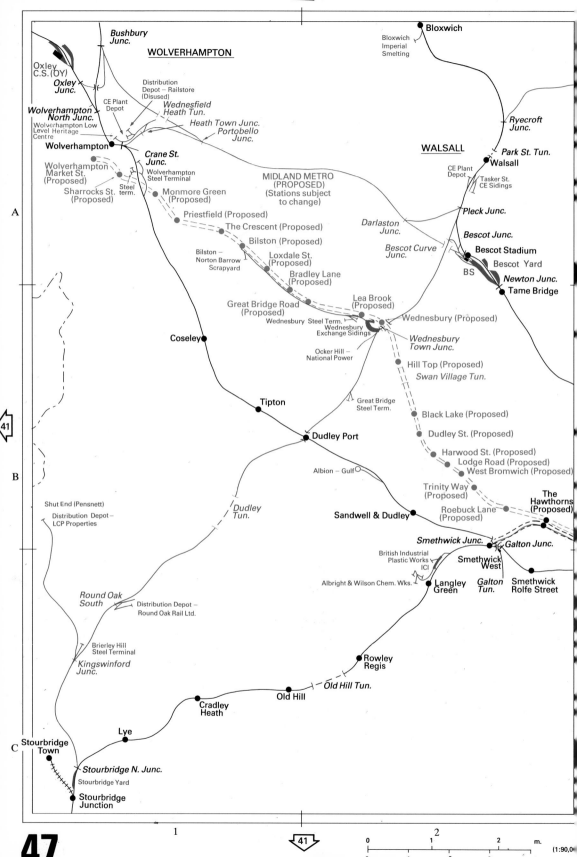

**WOLVERHAMPTON**

*Bushbury Junc.*

*Oxley C.S. (OY)*
*Oxley Junc.*

Bloxwich

Bloxwich Imperial Smelting

*Wolverhampton North Junc.*
Wolverhampton Low Level Heritage Centre

Distribution Depot – Railstore (Disused)

CE Plant Depot

*Wednesfield Heath Tun.*

Heath Town Junc.
*Portobello Junc.*

*Ryecroft Junc.*

**WALSALL**

Wolverhampton

*Crane St. Junc.*

Wolverhampton Steel Terminal

Wolverhampton Market St. (Proposed)

Sharrocks St. (Proposed)

Steel term.

Monmore Green (Proposed)

MIDLAND METRO (PROPOSED) (Stations subject to change)

*Park St. Tun.*
Walsall

CE Plant Depot

Tasker St. CE Sidings

*Pleck Junc.*

*Darlaston Junc.*

*Bescot Junc.*

Priestfield (Proposed)

The Crescent (Proposed)

Bilston (Proposed)

Bilston – Norton Barrow Scrapyard

Loxdale St. (Proposed)

Bradley Lane (Proposed)

*Bescot Curve Junc.*

**Bescot Stadium**

Bescot Yard

BS

*Newton Junc.*
Tame Bridge

Great Bridge Road (Proposed)

Lea Brook (Proposed)

Wednesbury (Proposed)

Wednesbury Steel Term.
Wednesbury Exchange Sidings

*Wednesbury Town Junc.*

**Coseley**

Ocker Hill – National Power

Hill Top (Proposed)
*Swan Village Tun.*

**Tipton**

Great Bridge Steel Term.

**Dudley Port**

Black Lake (Proposed)

Dudley St. (Proposed)

Albion – Gulf

Harwood St. (Proposed)
Lodge Road (Proposed)
West Bromwich (Proposed)

Trinity Way (Proposed)

Roebuck Lane (Proposed)

The Hawthorns (Proposed)

Shut End (Pensnett)
Distribution Depot – LCP Properties

*Dudley Tun.*

**Sandwell & Dudley**

*Smethwick Junc.*
*Galton Junc.*

British Industrial Plastic Works
ICI

Albright & Wilson Chem. Wks.

Smethwick West

*Galton Tun.*

Smethwick Rolfe Street

*Round Oak South*

Distribution Depot – Round Oak Rail Ltd.

Langley Green

Brierley Hill Steel Terminal

*Kingswinford Junc.*

Rowley Regis

*Old Hill Tun.*

**Stourbridge Town**

Lye

Cradley Heath

Old Hill

*Stourbridge N. Junc.*

Stourbridge Yard

**Stourbridge Junction**

A

B

C

41

41

47

1

2

0          1          2    m.
0    1    2    3    4 km.

(1:90,0

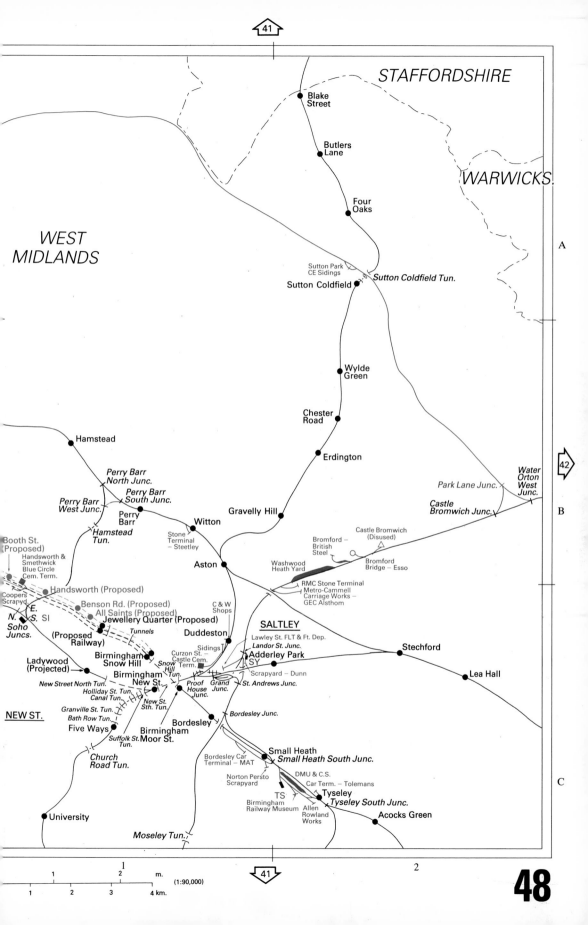

STAFFORDSHIRE

WARWICKS.

Blake
Street

Butlers
Lane

Four
Oaks

WEST
MIDLANDS

A

Sutton Park
CE Sidings

*Sutton Coldfield Tun.*

Sutton Coldfield

Wylde
Green

Chester
Road

Erdington

Water
Orton
West
Junc.

*Park Lane Junc.*

42

*Castle
Bromwich Junc.*

B

Hamstead

*Perry Barr
North Junc.*

*Perry Barr
South Junc.*

*Perry Barr
West Junc.*

Perry
Barr

Witton

Gravelly Hill

*Hamstead
Tun.*

Stone
Terminal
– Steetley

Aston

Bromford –
British
Steel

Castle Bromwich
(Disused)

Bromford
Bridge – Esso

Washwood
Heath Yard

Booth St.
(Proposed)

Handsworth &
Smethwick
Blue Circle
Cem. Term.

Coopers
Scrapyd.

Handsworth (Proposed)

Benson Rd. (Proposed)

All Saints (Proposed)

Jewellery Quarter (Proposed)

RMC Stone Terminal
Metro-Cammell
Carriage Works –
GEC Alsthom

C & W
Shops

E.
S. SI

N.
Soho
Juncs.

(Proposed)
Railway)

*Tunnels*

Duddeston

SALTLEY

Lawley St. FLT & Ft. Dep.

*Landor St. Junc.*

Stechford

Ladywood
(Projected)

Birmingham
Snow Hill

Sidings
Curzon St. –
Castle Cem.
Term.

*Snow
Hill
Tun.*

Adderley Park

SY

Lea Hall

Scrapyard – Dunn

*New Street North Tun.*

Birmingham
New St.

*Holliday St. Tun.
Canal Tun.*

*Proof
House
Junc.*

*Grand
Junc.*

*St. Andrews Junc.*

*New St.
Sth. Tun.*

NEW ST.

*Granville St. Tun.*
*Bath Row Tun.*

Five Ways

Bordesley

*Bordesley Junc.*

*Suffolk St.
Tun.*

Birmingham
Moor St.

*Church
Road Tun.*

Small Heath

*Small Heath South Junc.*

Bordesley Car
Terminal – MAT

Norton Persto
Scrapyard

DMU & C.S.

Car Term. – Tolemans

TS

Tyseley

*Tyseley South Junc.*

Birmingham
Railway Museum

Allen
Rowland
Works

Acocks Green

C

University

*Moseley Tun.*

1
2

1
2
m.
(1:90,000)

1
2
3
4 km.

2

**48**

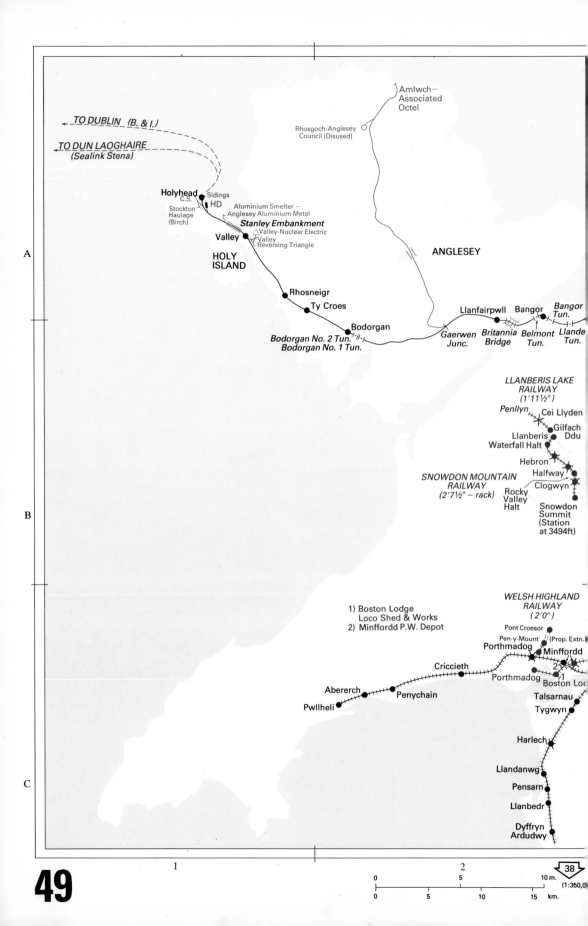

TO DUBLIN (B. & I.)

TO DUN LAOGHAIRE
(Sealink Stena)

Amlwch—
Associated
Octel

Rhosgoch-Anglesey
Council (Disused)

Holyhead
C.S.   Sidings
HD
Stockton
Haulage
(Birch)

Aluminium Smelter —
Anglesey Aluminium Metal

*Stanley Embankment*

Valley-Nuclear Electric
Valley
Valley
Reversing Triangle

ANGLESEY

**A**

HOLY
ISLAND

Rhosneigr

Ty Croes

Bodorgan

*Bodorgan No. 2 Tun.*
*Bodorgan No. 1 Tun.*

Llanfairpwll   Bangor   *Bangor*
*Tun.*

*Gaerwen*   *Britannia*   *Belmont*   *Llande*
*Junc.*   *Bridge*   *Tun.*   *Tun.*

*LLANBERIS LAKE*
*RAILWAY*
*(1'11½")*

*Penllyn*   Cei Llyden

Gilfach
Llanberis   Ddu
Waterfall Halt

Hebron

*SNOWDON MOUNTAIN*
*RAILWAY*
*(2'7½" — rack)*

Halfway
Clogwyn
Rocky
Valley
Halt
Snowdon
Summit
(Station
at 3494ft)

**B**

1) Boston Lodge
   Loco Shed & Works
2) Minffordd P.W. Depot

*WELSH HIGHLAND*
*RAILWAY*
*( 2'0″ )*

Pont Croesor
Pen-y-Mount   (Prop. Extn.)
Porthmadog   Minffordd

Criccieth   Porthmadog   Boston Loc

Abererch   Penychain   Talsarnau

Pwllheli   Tygwyn

Harlech

Llandanwg

**C**   Pensarn

Llanbedr

Dyffryn
Ardudwy

**49**

1

2

38

0   5   10 m.

0   5   10   15 km.

(1:350,0

GREAT ORME TRAMWAY
(ABERCONWY DISTRICT COUNCIL)
(3' 6")

Point of Ayr

Great Orme
Halfway
Llandudno Victoria
Llandudno
*Talacre*
Prestatyn

*Conwy Tubular Bridge*
*Penmaenbach Tun.*
C.S.
Deganwy
Rhyl

Penmaenmawr – ARC
LJ
Colwyn Bay
*Penmaenrhos Tun.*
A

*Penclip Tun.*
Llandudno Junc.
Abergele & Pensarn

Conwy
Penmaenmawr
Goods & Heron Oil

Llanfairfechan
Glan Conwy

Tal-y-Cafn

Dolgarrog

Llanrwst North
Llanrwst

CLWYD

51

Betws-y-Coed
B

Pont-y-Pant
*Beaverpool Tun.*

*Pont-y-Pant Upper Tun.*
*Pont-y-Pant Lower Tun.*
Dolwyddelan
Roman Bridge

*FFESTINIOG RAILWAY (1'11½")*

*Ffestiniog Tunnel (2m. 338yds.)*

Glan-y-Pwll Depot
Tan-y-Grisiau
Blaenau Ffestiniog

*LLANGOLLEN RAILWAY*

*Moelwyn Tun.*
Tan-y-Bwlch
Dduallt

Corwen
Carrog

w Goch
Campbells Platform
Plas Halt

Penrhyn
Penrhyndeudraeth
*Maentwrog Road – ICI Nobel*
△ Trawsfynydd – Nuclear Electric

(Extension to Carrog under construction. Further extension to Corwen is proposed)

Llandecwyn

*GWYNEDD*

Bala
Bryn Hynod
Glan Llyn Halt
Llangywair
Pentrepiod Halt
*BALA LAKE RAILWAY (1'11½")*
Llanuwchllyn
C

*POWYS*

39

1
5
10 m.
(1:350,000)
5
10
15
km.
2

**50**

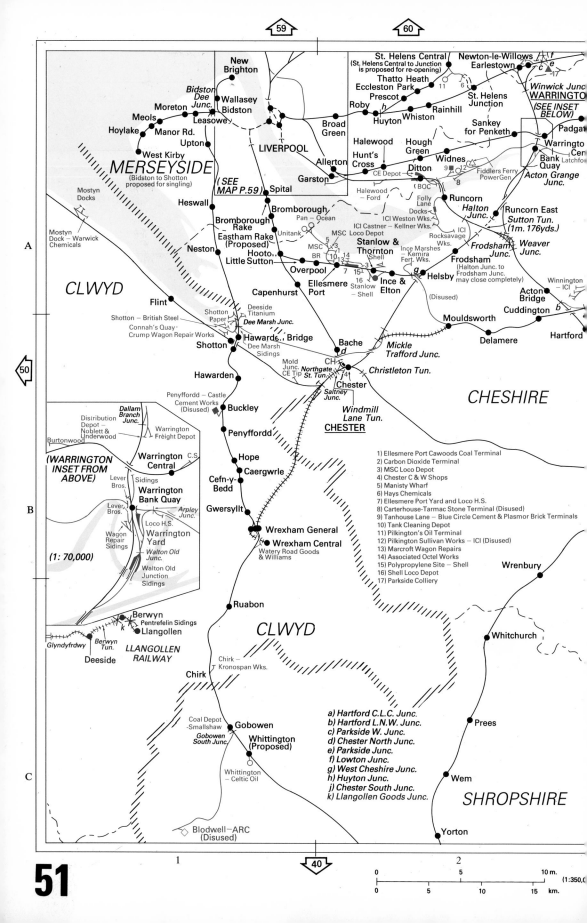

**MERSEYSIDE**
(Bidston to Shotton proposed for singling)

New Brighton

*Bidston Dee Junc.*
Wallasey
Bidston

Moreton
Meols
Leasowe
Hoylake
Manor Rd.
Upton
West Kirby

*(SEE MAP P.59)*
Spital

Mostyn Docks

Mostyn Dock – Warwick Chemicals

Heswall

Bromborough

Bromborough Rake
Eastham Rake
(Proposed)
Hooton
Little Sutton
Overpool
Ellesmere Port
Capenhurst

Neston

Pan – Ocean
Unitank

ICI Weston Wks.
ICI Castner – Kellner Wks.
MSC Loco Depot
MSC
BR
Stanlow & Thornton
Shell
Ince & Elton
Stanlow – Shell

St. Helens Central
(St. Helens Central to Junction is proposed for re-opening)
Thatto Heath
Eccleston Park
Prescot
Roby
Huyton
Whiston
Rainhill
Halewood
Hunt's Cross
Allerton
Garston
CE Depot
Halewood – Ford
Folly Lane Docks
BOC
Ditton
Widnes

Broad Green

**LIVERPOOL**

Newton-le-Willows
Earlestown
St. Helens Junction
Sankey for Penketh

*Winwick Junc.*
**WARRINGTON**
*(SEE INSET BELOW)*
Padgate
Warrington Cen.
Latchford
Bank Quay
*Acton Grange Junc.*

Fiddlers Ferry PowerGen

Runcorn
*Halton Junc.*
Runcorn East
*Sutton Tun.*
*(1m. 176yds.)*

Rocksavage Wks.
ICI
Ince Marshes – Kemira Fert. Wks.
*Frodsham Junc.*
Frodsham
(Halton Junc. to Frodsham Junc. may close completely)
Helsby
*West Cheshire Junc.*
Mouldsworth
Delamere
*Weaver Junc.*
Winnington – ICI
Acton Bridge
Cuddington
Hartford

**CLWYD**

Flint
Shotton Paper
Deeside Titanium
*Dee Marsh Junc.*
Shotton – British Steel
Connah's Quay –
Crump Wagon Repair Works
Hawarden Bridge
Dee Marsh Sidings
Shotton
Hawarden

Bache
*Mickle Trafford Junc.*
CH
Mold Junc.
CE Tip
*Northgate St. Tun.*
Chester
Saltney Junc.
*Windmill Lane Tun.*

**CHESTER**
*Christleton Tun.*

**CHESHIRE**

Penyffordd – Castle Cement Works (Disused)
Buckley
Penyffordd
Hope
Caergwrle
Cefn-y-Bedd
Gwersyllt
Wrexham General
Wrexham Central
Watery Road Goods & Williams

*(WARRINGTON INSET FROM ABOVE)*

Distribution Depot – Noblett & Underwood
Burtonwood
*Dallam Branch Junc.*
Warrington Freight Depot
Warrington Central
C.S.
Lever Bros.
Sidings
**Warrington Bank Quay**
Loco H.S.
Lever Bros.
Wagon Repair Sidings
Warrington Yard
*Arpley Junc.*
*Walton Old Junc.*
Walton Old Junction Sidings
**(1: 70,000)**

50

1) Ellesmere Port Cawoods Coal Terminal
2) Carbon Dioxide Terminal
3) MSC Loco Depot
4) Chester C & W Shops
5) Manisty Wharf
6) Hays Chemicals
7) Ellesmere Port Yard and Loco H.S.
8) Carterhouse-Tarmac Stone Terminal (Disused)
9) Tanhouse Lane – Blue Circle Cement & Plasmor Brick Terminals
10) Tank Cleaning Depot
11) Pilkington's Oil Terminal
12) Pilkington Sullivan Works – ICI (Disused)
13) Marcroft Wagon Repairs
14) Associated Octel Works
15) Polypropylene Site – Shell
16) Shell Loco Depot
17) Parkside Colliery

Wrenbury

Ruabon

Berwyn
Pentrefelin Sidings
Llangollen
Glyndyfrdwy
*Berwyn Tun.*
Deeside
**LLANGOLLEN RAILWAY**

**CLWYD**

Whitchurch

Chirk – Kronospan Wks.
Chirk

a) Hartford C.L.C. Junc.
b) Hartford L.N.W. Junc.
c) Parkside W. Junc.
d) Chester North Junc.
e) Parkside Junc.
f) Lowton Junc.
g) West Cheshire Junc.
h) Huyton Junc.
j) Chester South Junc.
k) Llangollen Goods Junc.

Prees

Coal Depot -Smallshaw
Gobowen
*Gobowen South Junc.*
Whittington (Proposed)
Whittington – Celtic Oil

Wem

**SHROPSHIRE**

Blodwell – ARC
(Disused)

Yorton

**51**

0   5   10 m.
(1:350,0
0   5   10   15 km.

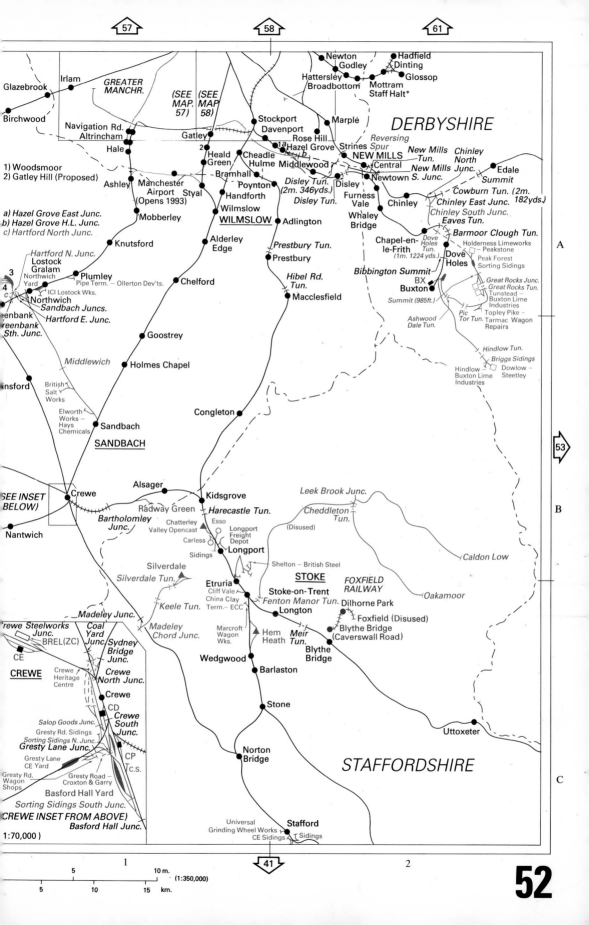

Glazebrook
Irlam
*GREATER MANCHR.*
Birchwood

Newton
Godley
Hadfield
Dinting
Hattersley
Broadbottom
Glossop
Mottram
Staff Halt*

(SEE MAP. 57)
(SEE MAP 58)

Navigation Rd.
Altrincham
Gatley
Stockport
Davenport
Rose Hill
Marple
**DERBYSHIRE**

Hale

Heald Green
Cheadle Hulme
Hazel Grove
Strines
*Reversing Spur*
New Mills
Tun.
New Mills
NEW MILLS
Central
New Mills
S. Junc.
Chinley North Junc.
Edale

1) Woodsmoor
2) Gatley Hill (Proposed)

Ashley
Manchester Airport Styal (Opens 1993)
Bramhall
Poynton
Handforth
Middlewood
*Disley Tun. (2m. 346yds.)*
Newtown
Disley
*Disley Tun.*
Furness Vale
Chinley
*Summit*
*Cowburn Tun. (2m. 182yds.)*
*Chinley East Junc.*

a) Hazel Grove East Junc.
b) Hazel Grove H.L. Junc.
c) Hartford North Junc.

Mobberley
Wilmslow
**WILMSLOW**
Adlington
Whaley Bridge
*Chinley South Junc.*
*Eaves Tun.*
*Barmoor Clough Tun.*

*Hartford N. Junc.*
Lostock Gralam
Northwich Yard
Knutsford
Alderley Edge
Prestbury
*Prestbury Tun.*
Chapel-en-le-Frith
*Dove Holes Tun. (1m. 1224yds.)*
Holderness Limeworks – Peakstone
Peak Forest Sorting Sidings

3
Northwich
*ICI Lostock Wks.*
Plumley
*Pipe Term. — Ollerton Dev'ts.*
Chelford
*Bibbington Summit*
BX
Buxton
Dove Holes
*Great Rocks Junc.*
*Great Rocks Tun.*
Tunstead – Buxton Lime Industries

4
*Sandbach Juncs.*
*Hartford E. Junc.*
*Summit (985ft.)*
Topley Pike – Tarmac Wagon Repairs

enbank
reenbank
Sth. Junc.
Goostrey
*Hibel Rd. Tun.*
Macclesfield
*Ashwood Dale Tun.*
*Pic Tor Tun.*

*Middlewich*
Holmes Chapel
*Hindlow Tun.*
*Briggs Sidings*
Hindlow Buxton Lime Industries
Dowlow Steetley

nsford
*British Salt Works*
*Elworth Works — Hays Chemicals*
Congleton

Sandbach
**SANDBACH**

Alsager
Kidsgrove
*Leek Brook Junc.*

SEE INSET BELOW)
Crewe
Radway Green
*Harecastle Tun.*
*Cheddleton Tun.*

Nantwich
*Bartholomley Junc.*
Chatterley Valley Opencast
Esso
Carless
Longport Freight Depot
(Disused)
Caldon Low

Sidings
Longport
Shelton – British Steel
**STOKE**
**FOXFIELD RAILWAY**
Oakamoor

Silverdale
*Silverdale Tun.*
Etruria
Stoke-on-Trent
Cliff Vale
China Clay Term. – ECC
*Fenton Manor Tun.*
Longton
Dilhorne Park
Foxfield (Disused)

*Madeley Junc.*
*Coal Yard Junc.*
Crewe Steelworks Junc.
BREL(ZC)
*Keele Tun.*
*Madeley Chord Junc.*
Marcroft Wagon Wks.
Hem Heath
*Meir Tun.*
Blythe Bridge (Caverswall Road)

CE
*Sydney Bridge Junc.*
Crewe Heritage Centre
Wedgwood
Blythe Bridge

**CREWE**
*Crewe North Junc.*
Barlaston

CD
Crewe
Stone

*Salop Goods Junc.*
*Crewe South Junc.*
Gresty Rd. Sidings
*Sorting Sidings N. Junc.*
*Gresty Lane Junc.*
Gresty Lane CE Yard
CP
T.C.S.
Norton Bridge
**STAFFORDSHIRE**

Gresty Rd. Wagon Shops
Gresty Road – Croxton & Garry
Basford Hall Yard
*Sorting Sidings South Junc.*
CREWE INSET FROM ABOVE)
*Basford Hall Junc.*

Uttoxeter

1:70,000 )

Universal Grinding Wheel Works
CE Sidings
Stafford
Sidings

1          10 m.
5                    (1:350,000)
5      10      15 km.

2

**52**

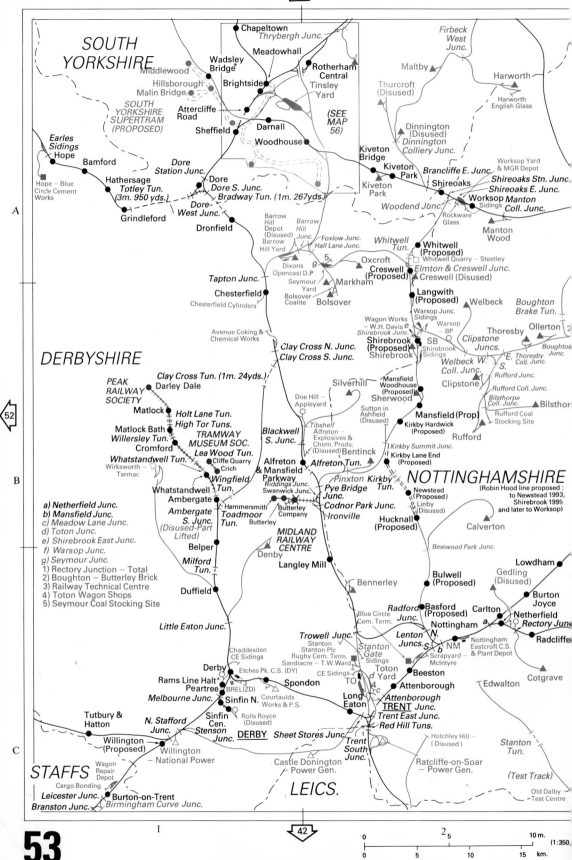

SOUTH YORKSHIRE

Chapeltown
Thrybergh Junc.
Meadowhall
Wadsley Bridge*
Middlewood
Hillsborough
Malin Bridge
Brightside
Rotherham Central
Tinsley Yard

Firbeck West Junc.
Maltby
Harworth

Thurcroft (Disused)
Harworth English Glass

Attercliffe Road
Sheffield
Darnall
SOUTH YORKSHIRE SUPERTRAM (PROPOSED)

Woodhouse

(SEE MAP 56)

Dinnington (Disused)
Dinnington Colliery Junc.

Kiveton Bridge
Kiveton Park
Kiveton Park

Brancliffe E. Junc.
Shireoaks
Shireoaks Stn. Junc.
Shireoaks E. Junc.
Worksop Yard & MGR Depot

Earles Sidings
Hope
Bamford
Hathersage
Totley Tun. (3m. 950 yds.)
Dore Station Junc.
Dore
Dore S. Junc.
Bradway Tun. (1m. 267yds.)

Woodend Junc.
Worksop
Sidings
Manton Coll. Junc.
Rockware Glass
Manton Wood

Hope – Blue Circle Cement Works
Grindleford
Dore West Junc.
Dronfield

Barrow Hill Depot (Disused)
Barrow Hill Yard
Barrow Hill Junc.
Foxlow Junc.
Hall Lane Junc.
Whitwell Tun.
Whitwell (Proposed)
Whitwell Quarry – Steetley

DERBYSHIRE

Tapton Junc.
Dixons Opencast D.P
Seymour Yard
Bolsover Coalite
Markham
Bolsover
g
Oxcroft
Creswell (Proposed)
Elmton & Creswell Junc.
Creswell (Disused)

Langwith (Proposed)
Welbeck
Boughton Brake Tun.

Chesterfield
Chesterfield Cylinders

Warsop Junc. Sidings
Wagon Works – W.H. Davis
Shirebrook Junc.
Shirebrook (Proposed)
Shirebrook
Thoresby
Ollerton

Avenue Coking & Chemical Works
Clay Cross N. Junc.
Clay Cross S. Junc.

e
f
Warsop
BP
SB
Shirebrook Sidings
Welbeck W. Coll. Junc.
Clipstone Juncs.
E. Thoresby Coll. Junc.
Boughton Junc.

PEAK RAILWAY SOCIETY
Clay Cross Tun. (1m. 24yds.)
Darley Dale

Silverhill
Mansfield Woodhouse (Proposed)
Sherwood

Clipstone
Rufford Coll. Junc.
Bilsthorpe Coll. Junc.
Rufford Coal Stocking Site
Bilsthor

Matlock
Holt Lane Tun.
High Tor Tuns.
Matlock Bath
Willersley Tun.
Cromford
TRAMWAY MUSEUM SOC.
Lea Wood Tun.
Whatstandwell Tun.
Wirksworth – Tarmac
Cliffe Quarry
Crich

Blackwell S. Junc.
Doe Hill – Appleyard
Tibshelf
Alfreton – Explosives & Chem. Prods. (Disused)
Bentinck

Sutton in Ashfield (Disused)
Kirkby Hardwick
Mansfield (Prop)
Kirkby Hardwick (Proposed)
Rufford

Kirkby Summit Junc.
Kirkby Lane End (Proposed)

NOTTINGHAMSHIRE
(Robin Hood line proposed : to Newstead 1993, Shirebrook 1995 and later to Worksop)

Alfreton & Mansfield Parkway
Wingfield Tun.
Whatstandwell
Ambergate
Ambergate S. Junc. (Disused-Part Lifted)
Riddings Junc.
Swanwick Junc.
Hammersmith
Toadmoor Tun.
Butterley
Butterley Company
Alfreton Tun.
Pinxton
Pye Bridge Junc.
Codnor Park Junc.
Ironville
Kirkby Tun.
Newstead (Proposed)
Linby (Disused)
Hucknall (Proposed)

Calverton

a) Netherfield Junc.
b) Mansfield Junc.
c) Meadow Lane Junc.
d) Toton Junc.
e) Shirebrook East Junc.
f) Warsop Junc.
g) Seymour Junc.
1) Rectory Junction – Total
2) Boughton – Butterley Brick
3) Railway Technical Centre
4) Toton Wagon Shops
5) Seymour Coal Stocking Site

Belper
Milford Tun.
Duffield

MIDLAND RAILWAY CENTRE
Denby
Langley Mill
Bennerley
Blue Circle Cem. Term.
Radford Junc.
Basford (Proposed)
Bestwood Park Junc.
Bulwell (Proposed)

Lowdham
Gedling (Disused)
Burton Joyce
Carlton
Netherfield
Rectory Jun
Radcliffe

Little Eaton Junc.
Trowell Junc.
Stanton
Stanton Plc
Rugby Cem. Term.
Sandiacre – T.W.Ward
CE Sidings
Stanton Gate
Lenton Juncs.
Nottingham
N.
Nottingham Eastcroft C.S. & Plant Depot
Scrapyard
McIntyre
Cotgrave
Edwalton

Chaddesden CE Sidings
Derby
Etches Pk. C.S. (DY)
Rams Line Halt*
Peartree
BREL(ZD)
Melbourne Junc.
Sinfin N.
Spondon
Courtaulds Works & P.S.
NM
S.
b
TO
Toton Yard
Beeston
Attenborough

Tutbury & Hatton
N. Stafford Junc.
Sinfin Cen.
Stenson Junc.
DERBY
Rolls Royce (Disused)
Long Eaton
Attenborough Junc.
TRENT Junc.
Trent East Junc.
Red Hill Tuns.
Stanton Tun.

STAFFS
Willington (Proposed)
Wagon Repair Depot
Cargo Bonding
Willington – National Power
Sheet Stores Junc.
Castle Donington – Power Gen.
Trent South Junc.
Hotchley Hill – (Disused)
Ratcliffe-on-Soar – Power Gen.
Stanton Tun.
(Test Track)

Leicester Junc.
Branston Junc.
Burton-on-Trent
Birmingham Curve Junc.
LEICS.
Old Dalby Test Centre

1

0        5        10 m.
(1:350)
0    5    10    15 km.

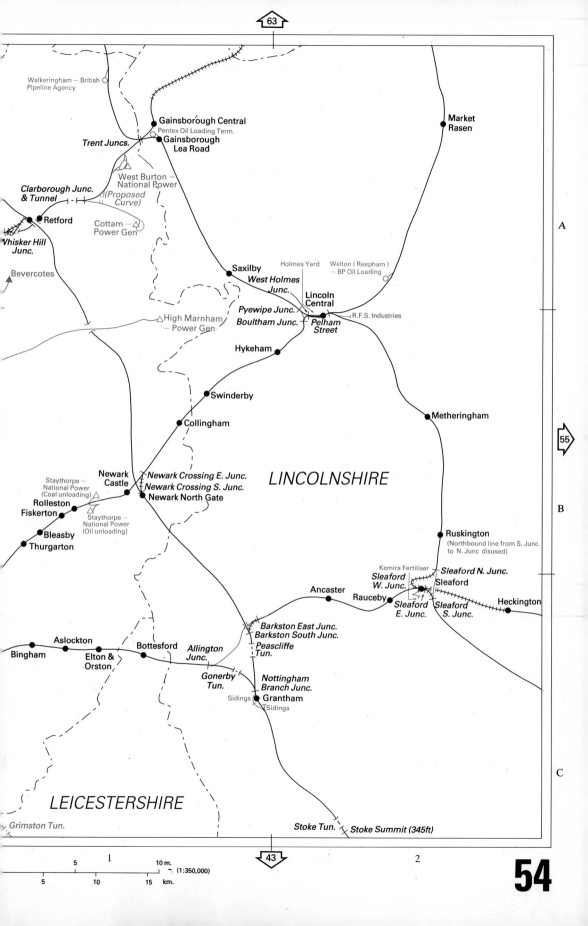

Walkeringham – British
Pipeline Agency

Gainsborough Central
Pentex Oil Loading Term.
Gainsborough
Lea Road

Market
Rasen

*Trent Juncs.*

West Burton –
National Power

*Clarborough Junc.
& Tunnel*

*(Proposed
Curve)*

Retford

Cottam –
Power Gen

*Whisker Hill
Junc.*

Bevercotes

Saxilby

Holmes Yard

Welton ( Reepham )
– BP Oil Loading

*West Holmes
Junc.*

Lincoln
Central

*Pyewipe Junc.*

*Boultham Junc.*

Pelham
Street

R.F.S. Industries

△High Marnham
– Power Gen

Hykeham

Swinderby

Metheringham

Collingham

LINCOLNSHIRE

Newark
Castle

*Newark Crossing E. Junc.*

*Newark Crossing S. Junc.*

Newark North Gate

Staythorpe –
National Power
(Coal unloading) △

Rolleston
Fiskerton

Staythorpe –
National Power
(Oil unloading)

Bleasby
Thurgarton

Ruskington

(Northbound line from S. Junc.
to N. Junc disused)

Kemira Fertiliser

*Sleaford N. Junc.*

*Sleaford
W. Junc.*

Sleaford

Ancaster

Rauceby

*Sleaford
E. Junc.*

*Sleaford
S. Junc.*

Heckington

Aslockton

Bottesford

*Allington
Junc.*

*Barkston East Junc.*

*Barkston South Junc.*

*Peascliffe
Tun.*

Bingham

Elton &
Orston

*Gonerby
Tun.*

*Nottingham
Branch Junc.*

Sidings

Grantham

Sidings

LEICESTERSHIRE

*Grimston Tun.*

*Stoke Tun.*

Stoke Summit (345ft)

5   1   10 m.

(1:350,000)

5   10   15   km.

2

A

55

B

C

**54**

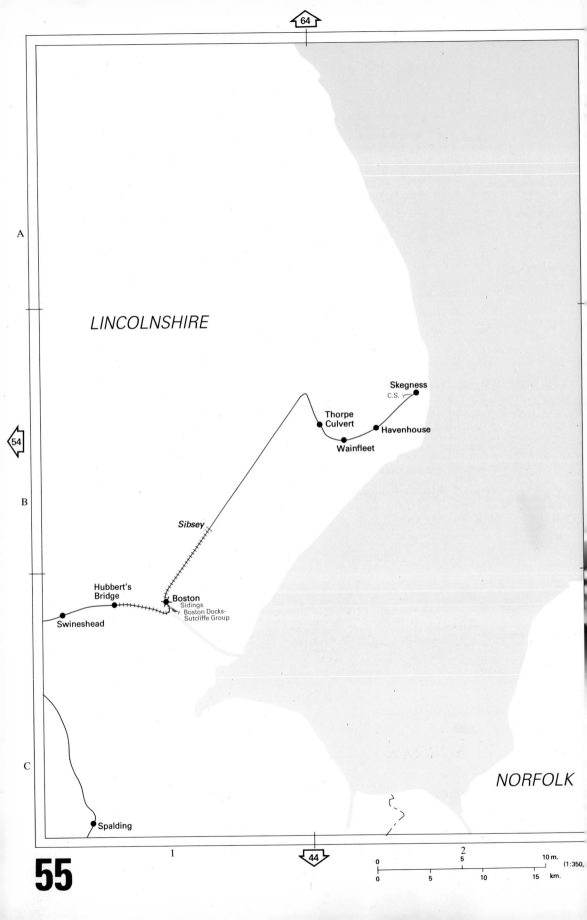

64

LINCOLNSHIRE

54

A

B

C

Skegness
C.S.

Thorpe
Culvert

Havenhouse

Wainfleet

Sibsey

Hubbert's
Bridge

Boston
Sidings
Boston Docks-
Sutcliffe Group

Swineshead

NORFOLK

Spalding

1

44

2
5

10 m.

(1:350,

0
0        5        10        15   km.

**55**

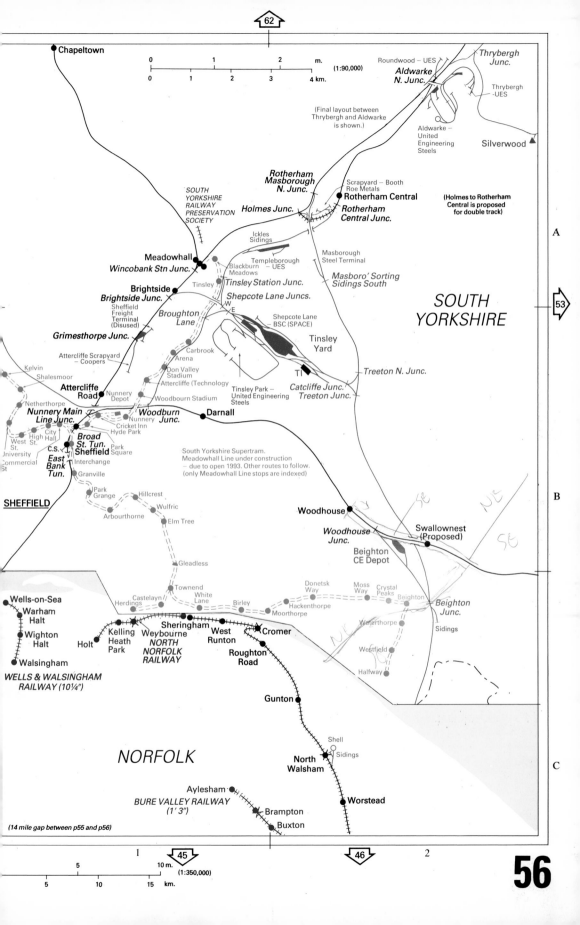

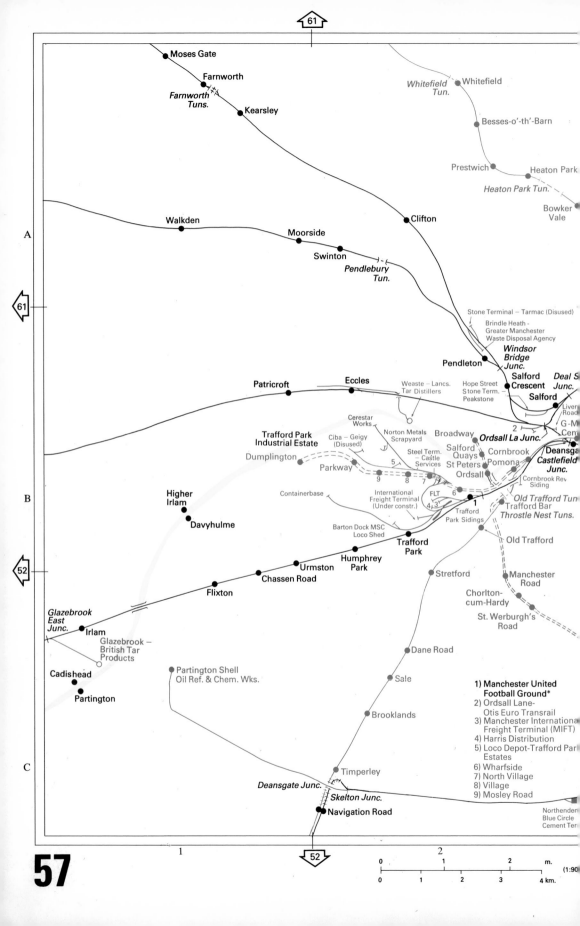

Moses Gate

Farnworth

*Farnworth Tuns.*

Kearsley

Whitefield Tun.

Whitefield

Besses-o'-th'-Barn

Prestwich

Heaton Park

*Heaton Park Tun.*

Bowker Vale

Walkden

Clifton

Moorside

Swinton

*Pendlebury Tun.*

**A**

Stone Terminal – Tarmac (Disused)

Brindle Heath – Greater Manchester Waste Disposal Agency

*Windsor Bridge Junc.*

Pendleton

*Deal S Junc.*

Patricroft

Eccles

Weaste – Lancs. Tar Distillers

Hope Street Stone Term. Peakstone

Salford Crescent

Salford

Liver Road

*Ordsall La Junc.*

G-M Cen

Cerestar Works

Broadway

Trafford Park Industrial Estate

Ciba – Geigy (Disused)

Norton Metals Scrapyard

Salford Quays

St Peters

Cornbrook

Pomona

Deansga

*Castlefield Junc.*

Dumplington

Parkway

Steel Term. – Castle Services

Ordsall

Cornbrook Rev Siding

5

9     8     7

6

*Old Trafford Tun*

Trafford Bar

*Throstle Nest Tuns.*

**B**

Higher Irlam

Davyhulme

Containerbase

International Freight Terminal (Under constr.)

FLT

4  3

1

Trafford Park Sidings

Barton Dock MSC Loco Shed

Trafford Park

Old Trafford

Humphrey Park

Urmston

Chassen Road

Stretford

Manchester Road

Chorlton-cum-Hardy

Flixton

St. Werburgh's Road

**52**

*Glazebrook East Junc.*

Irlam

Glazebrook – British Tar Products

Dane Road

Cadishead

Sale

Partington

Partington Shell Oil Ref. & Chem. Wks.

Brooklands

1) **Manchester United Football Ground***

2) Ordsall Lane- Otis Euro Transrail

3) Manchester International Freight Terminal (MIFT)

4) Harris Distribution

5) Loco Depot-Trafford Par Estates

6) Wharfside

7) North Village

8) Village

9) Mosley Road

**C**

Timperley

*Deansgate Junc.*

*Skelton Junc.*

Navigation Road

Northenden Blue Circle Cement Ter

1

2

0           1           2      m.

0     1     2     3     4 km.

(1:90

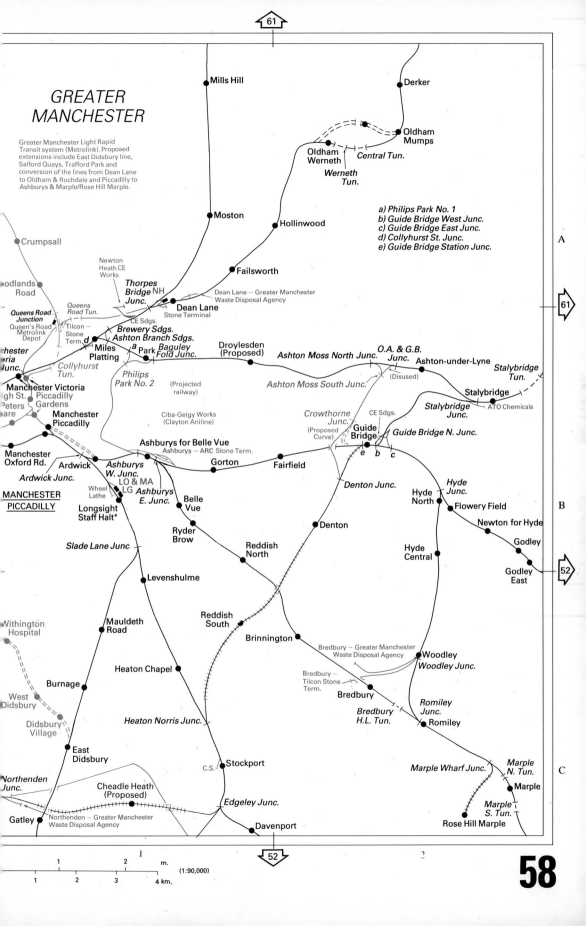

# GREATER MANCHESTER

Greater Manchester Light Rapid
Transit system (Metrolink). Proposed
extensions include East Didsbury line,
Salford Quays, Trafford Park and
conversion of the lines from Dean Lane
to Oldham & Rochdale and Piccadilly to
Ashburys & Marple/Rose Hill Marple.

Mills Hill

Derker

Oldham
Mumps

Oldham
Werneth  *Central Tun.*

*Werneth
Tun.*

Moston

Hollinwood

a) *Philips Park No. 1*
b) *Guide Bridge West Junc.*
c) *Guide Bridge East Junc.*
d) *Collyhurst St. Junc.*
e) *Guide Bridge Station Junc.*

A

61

Crumpsall

Failsworth

Newton
Heath CE
Works

odlands
Road

*Thorpes
Bridge* NH
*Junc.*

Dean Lane — Greater Manchester
Waste Disposal Agency

*Queens Road
Junction*

*Queens
Road Tun.*

Dean Lane
Stone Terminal

CE Sdgs.

Queen's Road
Metrolink
Depot

Tilcon –
Stone
Term.

d

*Brewery Sdgs.*
*Ashton Branch Sdgs.*

hester
ria
unc.

*Collyhurst
Tun.*

Miles
Platting

a

Park

*Baguley
Fold Junc.*

Droylesden
(Proposed)

*Ashton Moss North Junc.*

*O.A. & G.B.
Junc.*

Ashton-under-Lyne

*Stalybridge
Tun.*

gh St.
Peters
are

Manchester Victoria

*Philips
Park No. 2*

(Projected
railway)

*Ashton Moss South Junc.*

(Disused)

Stalybridge

Piccadilly
Gardens

ATO Chemicals

Manchester
Piccadilly

Ciba-Geigy Works
(Clayton Aniline)

*Crowthorne
Junc.*

*Stalybridge
Junc.*

*Guide Bridge N. Junc.*

Manchester
Oxford Rd.

Ardwick

Ashburys for Belle Vue

Ashburys – ARC Stone Term.

(Proposed
Curve)

Guide
Bridge

CE Sdgs.

*Ardwick Junc.*

*Ashburys
W. Junc.*

Gorton

Fairfield

e  b  c

*Hyde
Junc.*

B

### MANCHESTER
### PICCADILLY

LO & MA

Wheel
Lathe

LG  *Ashburys
E. Junc.*

Belle
Vue

*Denton Junc.*

Hyde
North

Flowery Field

Longsight
Staff Halt*

Newton for Hyde

*Slade Lane Junc.*

Ryder
Brow

Reddish
North

Denton

Hyde
Central

Godley

Levenshulme

Godley
East

52

Withington
Hospital

Mauldeth
Road

Reddish
South

Brinnington

Bredbury – Greater Manchester
Waste Disposal Agency

Woodley

*Woodley Junc.*

Heaton Chapel

Bredbury –
Tilcon Stone
Term.

Burnage

*Romiley
Junc.*

West
Didsbury

Bredbury

*Heaton Norris Junc.*

*Bredbury
H.L. Tun.*

Romiley

Didsbury
Village

East
Didsbury

C.S.

Stockport

*Marple Wharf Junc.*

*Marple
N. Tun.*

C

*Northenden
Junc.*

Cheadle Heath
(Proposed)

Marple

Gatley

Northenden – Greater Manchester
Waste Disposal Agency

*Edgeley Junc.*

*Marple
S. Tun.*

Davenport

Rose Hill Marple

1        2        m.

1      2      3      4 km.

(1:90,000)

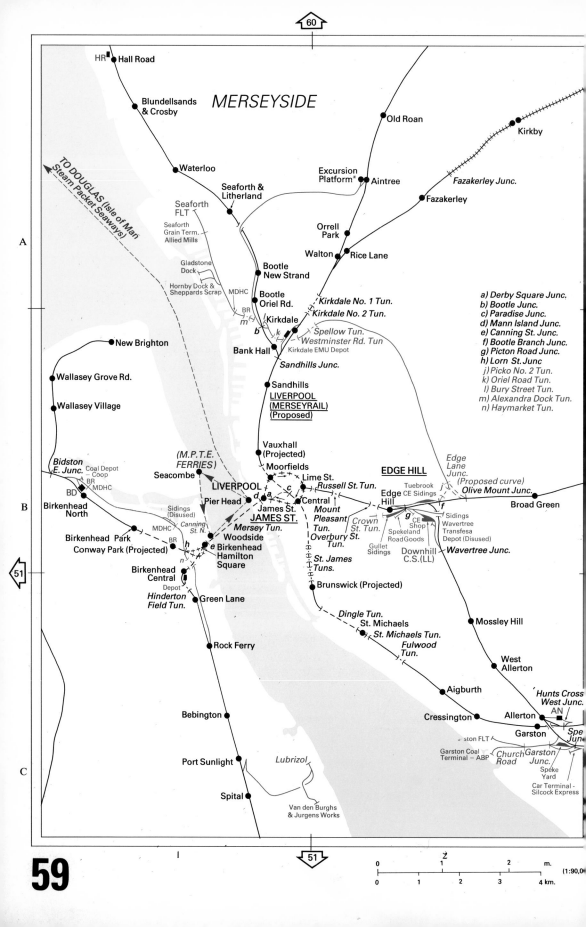

HR ■ Hall Road

Blundellsands & Crosby

**MERSEYSIDE**

Old Roan

Kirkby

Waterloo

*Fazakerley Junc.*

Seaforth & Litherland

Excursion Platform*  Aintree

Fazakerley

Seaforth FLT

Orrell Park

Seaforth Grain Term. Allied Mills

Walton  Rice Lane

Gladstone Dock

Bootle New Strand

Hornby Dock & Sheppards Scrap

MDHC

Bootle Oriel Rd.

*Kirkdale No. 1 Tun.*

BR
m

Kirkdale

*Kirkdale No. 2 Tun.*

b  k

*Spellow Tun.*

*Westminster Rd. Tun*

New Brighton

Bank Hall

Kirkdale EMU Depot

Wallasey Grove Rd.

*Sandhills Junc.*

Wallasey Village

Sandhills

**LIVERPOOL (MERSEYRAIL) (Proposed)**

Vauxhall (Projected)

*(M.P.T.E. FERRIES)*

Moorfields

*Bidston E. Junc.*

Coal Depot – Coop

Seacombe

Lime St.

**EDGE HILL**

*Edge Lane Junc.*

*(Proposed curve)*

BR  MDHC
BD

LIVERPOOL

*Russell St. Tun.*

Tuebrook CE Sidings

*Olive Mount Junc.*

Birkenhead North

Pier Head

d a  c

Central

Edge Hill

f

Broad Green

Sidings (Disused)

James St.

g  CE Shop

Sidings Wavertree Transfesa Depot (Disused)

Canning St. N.

**JAMES ST.**

*Mount Pleasant Tun.*

*Crown St. Tun.*

Spekeland Road Goods

MDHC

BR

*Mersey Tun.*

Woodside

*Overbury St. Tun.*

**Downhill C.S.(LL)**

*Wavertree Junc.*

Birkenhead Park

h

e  Birkenhead Hamilton Square

Gullet Sidings

Conway Park (Projected)

n

Birkenhead Central

*St. James Tuns.*

Mossley Hill

Depot

*Hinderton Field Tun.*

Green Lane

Brunswick (Projected)

West Allerton

*Dingle Tun.*

Rock Ferry

St. Michaels

*St. Michaels Tun.*

*Fulwood Tun.*

Aigburth

*Hunts Cross West Junc.*

Bebington

Cressington

Allerton

AN

Garston

*Spe Jun*

Port Sunlight

*Lubrizol*

*Church Road*

Garston Junc.

ston FLT

Spital

Garston Coal Terminal – ABP

Speke Yard

Van den Burghs & Jurgens Works

Car Terminal - Silcock Express

a) Derby Square Junc.
b) Bootle Junc.
c) Paradise Junc.
d) Mann Island Junc.
e) Canning St. Junc.
f) Bootle Branch Junc.
g) Picton Road Junc.
h) Lorn St. Junc
j) Picko No. 2 Tun.
k) Oriel Road Tun.
l) Bury Street Tun.
m) Alexandra Dock Tun.
n) Haymarket Tun.

TO DOUGLAS (Isle of Man Steam Packet Seaways)

A

B

C

**59**

51

0        1        2        m.
0    1    2    3    4 km.

(1:90,0

Barrow
Roose

*(SEE INSET BELOW)*

Wennington

Bare Lane    *Hest Bank*
Morecambe    *Morecambe South Junc.*

Lancaster

*TO DOUGLAS (Isle of Man Steam Packet Seaways)*

Heysham Port    *Heysham Moss*

Heysham – Nuclear Electric

(1 : 90,000)
**(BARROW INSET FROM ABOVE)**

BW
C.S.    Barrow

Roose
*Salthouse Junc.*

(Disused)

Ramsden Dock – British Nuclear Fuels

*TO DOUGLAS (I of M S.P. Seaways)*

Knott End
Fleetwood
Fleetwood Ash St.

**LANCASHIRE**

Rossall
Thornton Gate
P.W. Yard    *Hillhouse ICI Power Station*

Cleveleys
Little Bispham
Burn Naze    Burn Naze – ICI

*BLACKPOOL & FLEETWOOD TRAMWAY (PRINCIPAL STOPS) – BLACKPOOL TRANSPORT*

Bispham
Cabin    C.S. (BP)

Poulton-le-Fylde

Talbot Sq.    Layton
Tower    Blackpool North
Manchester Sq.    Depot

Kirkham & Wesham

Salwick

Blackpool South
Pleasure Beach    Blackpool Pleasure Beach
Starr Gate    Squires Gate

CE Tip
CE Sidings

British Nuclear Fuels

St. Annes-on-the-Sea    Ansdell & Fairhaven    Moss Side

Lytham

Preston
*(SEE INSET TO LEFT)*
*Lostock Hall Junc.*    Bamber Bridge

Pleasington

Farington Curve Junc.    *Lostock Hall*    *Farington Junc.*

**PRESTON**
Croft St. C.S.    *Deepdale Tuns.*
*Fylde Junc.*
Petrofina
Lanfina
*Preston Docks*

Deepdale NFD Coal Depot & Blue Circle Cement Terminal Dock St. Sidings

Loco shed
*Fishergate Tun.*

Borough of Preston Exchange Sidings

Preston
*Preston S. Junc.*
P.O. Term.

**(PRESTON INSET FROM RIGHT) (1 : 70,000)**

a) Bamfurlong Sdgs. Junc.
b) Ince Moss Junc.
c) Springs Branch Junc.
d) Bamfurlong Junc.
e) Haydock Branch Junc.
f) Gerard's Bridge Junc.

Leyland
*Leyland – DAF (Disused)*    Leyland

*Euxton Junc.*
Chorley – Royal Ordnance (Euxton)
*Chorley Tun.*    Chorley

Croston

Southport Railway Centre    Meols Cop

Southport
C.S.

Birkdale

Hillside

Ainsdale

Horwich – Parkfield Foundry (Disused)

Adlington

Bescar Lane    Rufford
New Lane

Hoscar
Burscough Bridge
Burscough Junc.    Parbold

Wimpey Waste Disposal Terminal

Blackrod
*GREATER MANCHESTER*

1) Bamber Bridge CE Depot
2) Bamber Bridge – Bowker Distribution Depot
3) Wigan Canal CE Depot
4) Edge Green – Kelbit Bitumen

Appley Bridge
Gathurst    C.S.
*Upholland Tun.*    3

WIGAN

Hindley
Wallgate

Freshfield
Ormskirk

Formby
Aughton Park

Town Green

Orrell
Upholland    N.W.
Pemberton    SP    c    Ince    *Crow Nest Junc.*

Hightown

Rainford    Ince Moss CE Tip    b a    d

Maghull    Bryn    4    e

Hall Road
Old Roan

Kirkby    Garswood

**MERSEYSIDE**

Bickershaw

Cowley Hill – Pilkington Wks.    f    *Golborne Junc.*

0    5    10 m.
(1:350,000)
.5    10    15 km.

**60**

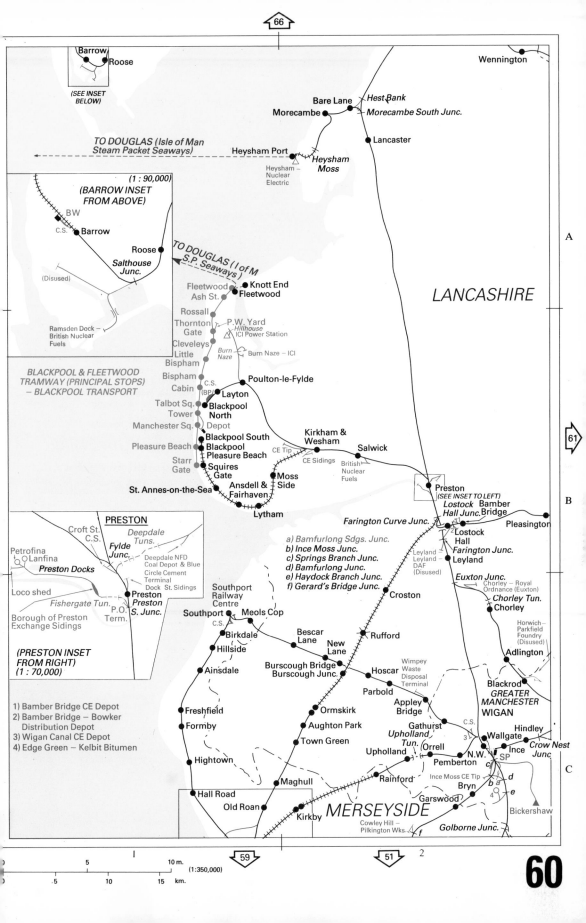

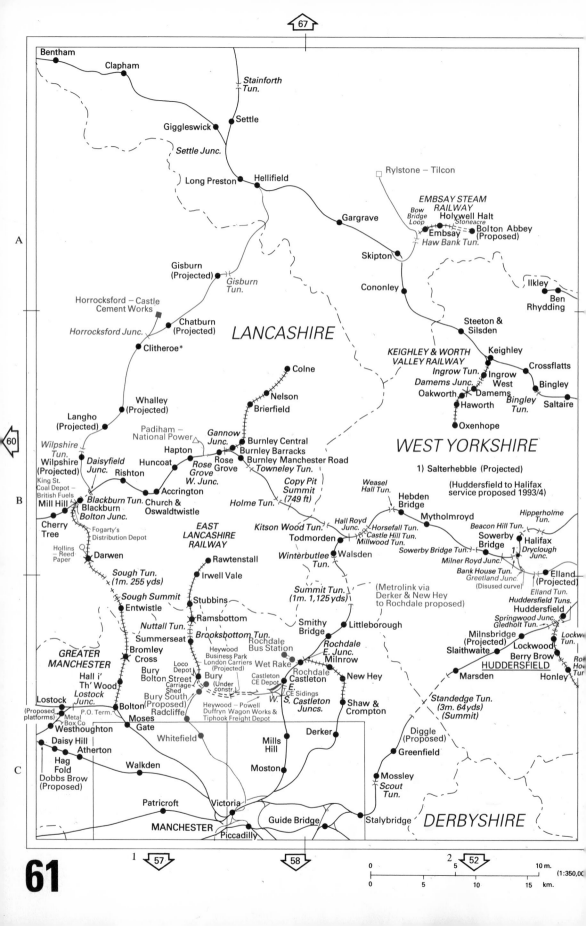

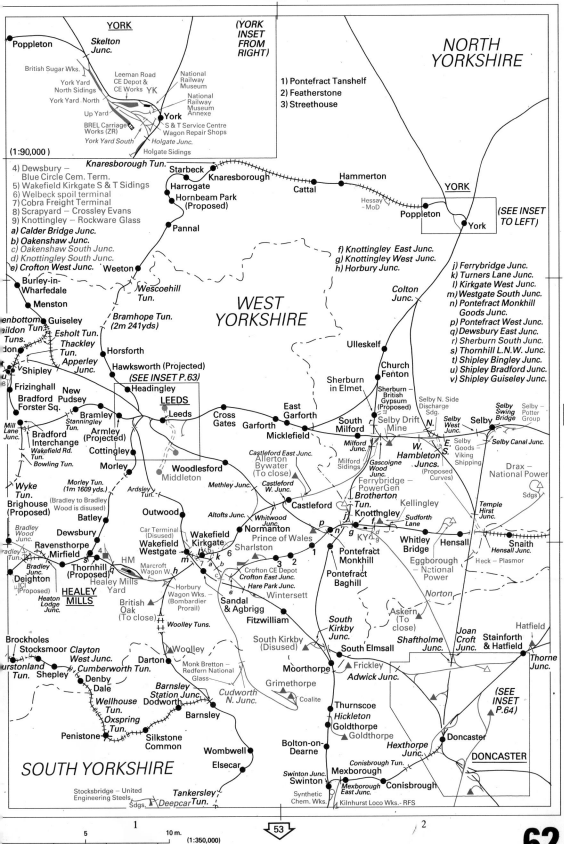

**YORK** *(YORK INSET FROM RIGHT)*

*Skelton Junc.*

Poppleton

British Sugar Wks.
Leeman Road CE Depot & CE Works
YK
National Railway Museum
York Yard North Sidings
National Railway Museum Annexe
York Yard North
Up Yard
York
BREL Carriage Works (ZR)
S & T Service Centre Wagon Repair Shops
*York Yard South*
*Holgate Junc.*
Holgate Sidings

(1:90,000)

1) Pontefract Tanshelf
2) Featherstone
3) Streethouse

*Knaresborough Tun.*

4) Dewsbury – Blue Circle Cem. Term.
5) Wakefield Kirkgate S & T Sidings
6) Welbeck spoil terminal
7) Cobra Freight Terminal
8) Scrapyard – Crossley Evans
9) Knottingley – Rockware Glass

a) Calder Bridge Junc.
b) Oakenshaw Junc.
c) Oakenshaw South Junc.
d) Knottingley South Junc.
e) Crofton West Junc.

f) Knottingley East Junc.
g) Knottingley West Junc.
h) Horbury Junc.

j) Ferrybridge Junc.
k) Turners Lane Junc.
l) Kirkgate West Junc.
m) Westgate Junc.
n) Pontefract Monkhill Goods Junc.
p) Pontefract West Junc.
q) Dewsbury East Junc.
r) Sherburn South Junc.
s) Thornhill L.N.W. Junc.
t) Shipley Bingley Junc.
u) Shipley Bradford Junc.
v) Shipley Guiseley Junc.

**NORTH YORKSHIRE**

**WEST YORKSHIRE**

**SOUTH YORKSHIRE**

Starbeck
Harrogate
Hornbeam Park (Proposed)
Pannal
Knaresborough
Cattal
Hammerton
Hessay – MoD
Poppleton
**YORK**
York
*(SEE INSET TO LEFT)*

Weeton
Burley-in-Wharfedale
Menston
*Wescoehill Tun.*
Colton Junc.
Ulleskelf
Church Fenton
Sherburn in Elmet
Sherburn – British Gypsum (Proposed)
Selby N. Side Discharge Sdg.
Selby Swing Bridge
Selby – Potter Group
Selby

*Bramhope Tun. (2m 241yds)*

Guiseley
*Esholt Tun.*
*Thackley Tun.*
*Apperley Junc.*
Horsforth
Hawksworth (Projected)
*(SEE INSET P.63)*
Headingley
**LEEDS**
Leeds

Shipley
Frizinghall
New Pudsey
Bradford Forster Sq.
Bramley
*Stanningley*
Armley (Projected)
Cottingley
Cross Gates
Garforth
East Garforth
Micklefield
South Milford
Milford Junc.
Milford Sidings
Selby West Junc.
Selby Goods – Viking Shipping
Selby Canal Junc.

Bradford Interchange
*Wakefield Rd. Tun.*
*Bowling Tun.*
Mill Lane Junc.
Morley
Woodlesford
Middleton
Castleford East Junc. (To close)
Allerton Bywater
Castleford W. Junc.
Gascoigne Wood Junc.
W. Hambleton Juncs.
E.S. (Proposed Curves)
Selby Drift Mine
N.
W.
Drax – National Power
Sdgs

*Wyke Tun.*
Brighouse (Proposed)
*Morley Tun. (1m 1609yds.)*
*Ardsley Tun.*
Methley Junc.
Altofts Junc.
Castleford
Whitwood Junc.
Normanton
Ferrybridge – PowerGen
*Brotherton Tun.*
Knottingley
Kellingley
Sudforth Lane
Temple Hirst Junc.

(Bradley to Bradley Wood is disused)
*Bradley Wood Junc.*
Batley
Dewsbury
Outwood
Car Terminal (Disused)
Prince of Wales
Sharlston
1
Whitley Bridge
Hensall
Snaith
Hensall Junc.

Ravensthorpe
Mirfield
Thornhill (Proposed)
*Bradley Junc.*
Deighton
[Cl] (Proposed)
Heaton Lodge Junc.
**HEALEY MILLS**
Healey Mills Yard
HM
Marcroft Wagon W.
Wakefield Westgate
Wakefield Kirkgate
6
m
7 a b
h
c
5
Sandal & Agbrigg
Crofton CE Depot
*Crofton East Junc.*
*Hare Park Junc.*
Wintersett
e
3 2
Pontefract Monkhill
Pontefract Baghill
p
n
j
g
q
KY
d
9
f
Eggborough – National Power
Norton
Askern (To close)
Joan Croft Junc.
Shaftholme Junc.
Heck – Plasmor

*Horbury Wagon Wks. – (Bombardier Prorail)*
British Oak (To close)
Fitzwilliam
South Kirkby Junc.
South Elmsall
Stainforth & Hatfield
Hatfield
Thorne Junc.
*(SEE INSET P.64)*

Brockholes
Stocksmoor
*Clayton West Junc.*
*Cumberworth Tun.*
*Woolley Tuns.*
Woolley
Darton
Monk Bretton – Redfern National Glass
South Kirkby (Disused)
Moorthorpe
Frickley
Adwick Junc.
Shepley
*Thurstonland Tun.*
Denby Dale
*Wellhouse Tun.*
*Oxspring Tun.*
Dodworth
Barnsley
*Barnsley Station Junc.*
*Cudworth N. Junc.*
Grimethorpe
Coalite
Thurnscoe
Hickleton
Goldthorpe
Doncaster
**DONCASTER**

Penistone
Silkstone Common
Wombwell
Elsecar
Bolton-on-Dearne
*Hexthorpe Junc.*

Stocksbridge – United Engineering Steels
Sdgs
*Tankersley Deepcar Tun.*
Mexborough
Swinton
*Swinton Junc.*
*Conisbrough Tun.*
Mexborough East Junc.
Conisbrough
Synthetic Chem. Wks.
Kilnhurst Loco Wks. – RFS

1
5       10 m.
(1:350,000)
5    10    15    km.

2

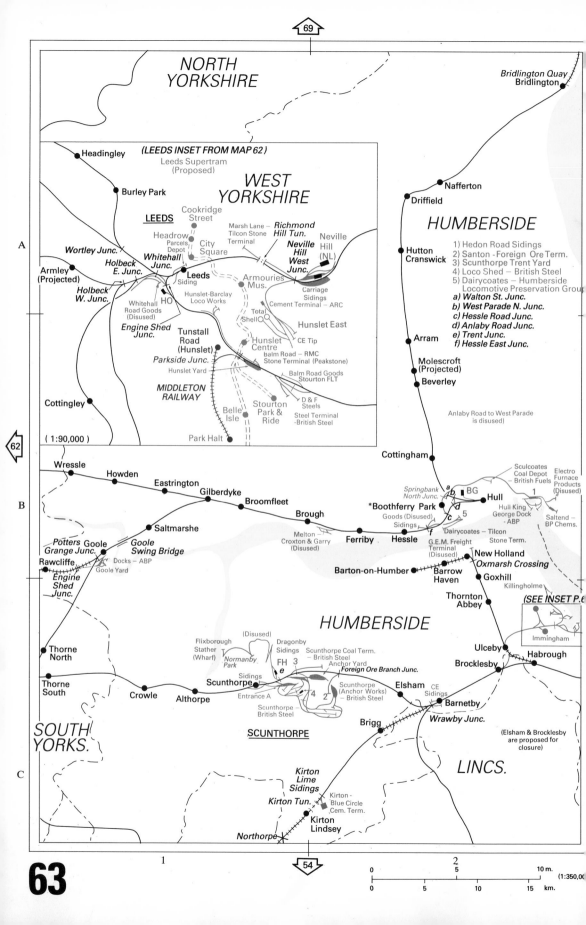

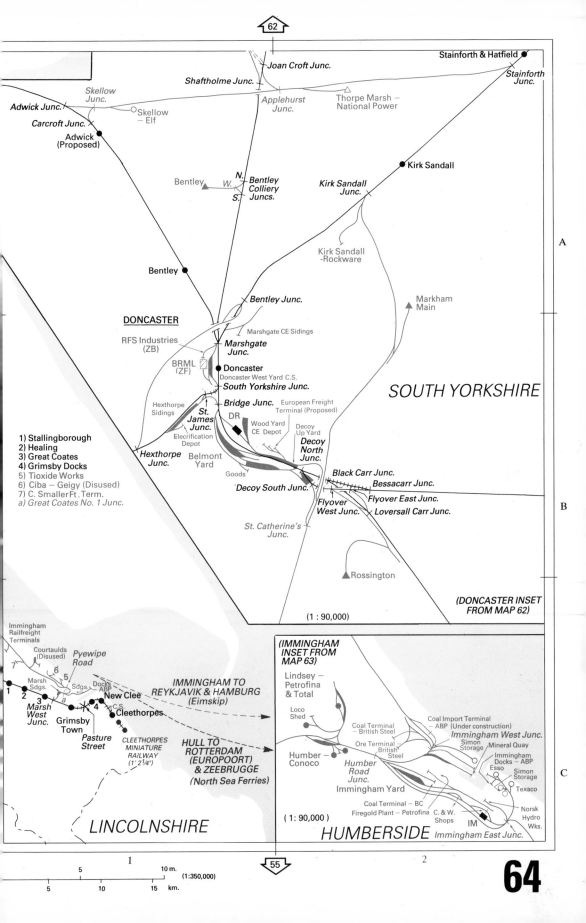

Stainforth & Hatfield

Joan Croft Junc.

Stainforth
Junc.

Shaftholme Junc.

Skellow
Junc.

Applehurst
Junc.

Thorpe Marsh –
National Power

Adwick Junc.

Skellow
– Elf

Carcroft Junc.

Adwick
(Proposed)

Kirk Sandall

A

Bentley

N.
W.
S.

Bentley
Colliery
Juncs.

Kirk Sandall
Junc.

Bentley

Kirk Sandall
-Rockware

Markham
Main

Bentley Junc.

**DONCASTER**

Marshgate CE Sidings

RFS Industries
(ZB)

Marshgate
Junc.

**SOUTH YORKSHIRE**

BRML
(ZF)

Doncaster

Doncaster West Yard C.S.

South Yorkshire Junc.

Hexthorpe
Sidings

Bridge Junc.

European Freight
Terminal (Proposed)

St.
James
Junc.

DR

Wood Yard
CE Depot

Decoy
Up Yard

1) Stallingborough
2) Healing
3) Great Coates
4) Grimsby Docks
5) Tioxide Works
6) Ciba – Geigy (Disused)
7) C. Smaller Ft. Term.
a) Great Coates No. 1 Junc.

Elecrification
Depot

Hexthorpe
Junc.

Belmont
Yard

Decoy
North
Junc.

Goods

Black Carr Junc.

Bessacarr Junc.

Decoy South Junc.

Flyover East Junc.

B

Flyover
West Junc.

Loversall Carr Junc.

St. Catherine's
Junc.

Rossington

(DONCASTER INSET
FROM MAP 62)

(1 : 90,000)

Immingham
Railfreight
Terminals

Courtaulds
(Disused)

Pyewipe
Road

6

5

Marsh
Sdgs.

Sdgs.

Docks
ABP

C.S.

New Clee

IMMINGHAM TO
REYKJAVIK & HAMBURG
(Eimskip)

(IMMINGHAM
INSET FROM
MAP 63)

Lindsey –
Petrofina
& Total

1

2

3

4

Cleethorpes

Loco
Shed

Coal Terminal
– British Steel

Coal Import Terminal
– ABP (Under construction)

Immingham West Junc.

Marsh
West
Junc.

a

Grimsby
Town

Pasture
Street

CLEETHORPES
MINIATURE
RAILWAY
(1' 2¼")

HULL TO
ROTTERDAM
(EUROPOORT)
& ZEEBRUGGE
(North Sea Ferries)

Ore Terminal –
British Steel

Simon
Storage

Mineral Quay

Humber
Conoco

Humber
Road
Junc.

Immingham Yard

Immingham
Docks – ABP

Esso

Simon
Storage

Texaco

Coal Terminal – BC

Firegold Plant – Petrofina

C. & W.
Shops

Norsk
Hydro
Wks.

C

IM

Immingham East Junc.

**LINCOLNSHIRE**

**HUMBERSIDE**

( 1 : 90,000 )

5

10 m.

(1:350,000)

5        10        15   km.

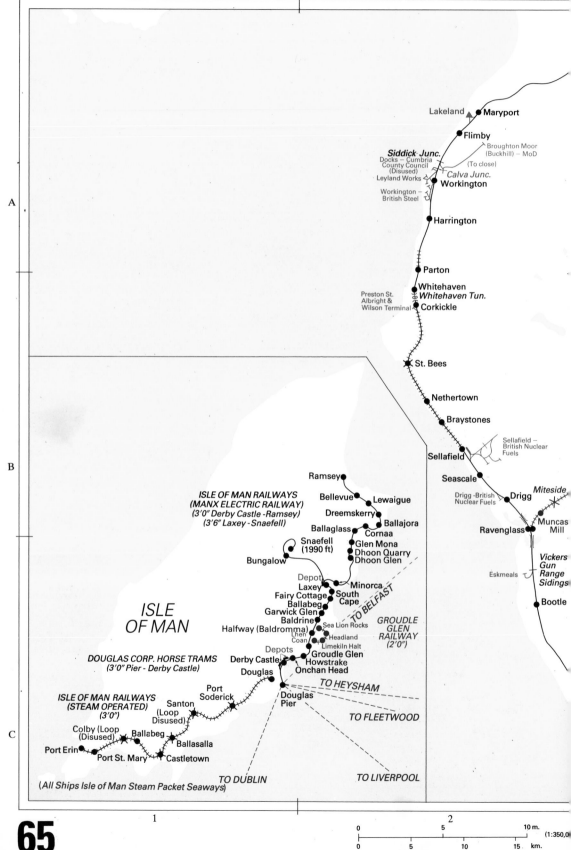

Lakeland ▲ ● Maryport

● Flimby

*Siddick Junc.*
Docks – Cumbria
County Council
(Disused)                    Broughton Moor
Leyland Works            (Buckhill) – MoD
                              (To close)
                         *Calva Junc.*
Workington –         ● Workington
British Steel

● Harrington

● Parton

● Whitehaven
*Whitehaven Tun.*
Preston St.
Albright &
Wilson Terminal    ● Corkickle

★ St. Bees

● Nethertown

● Braystones

Sellafield –
British Nuclear
Fuels
● Sellafield

Seascale ●

Drigg –British        *Miteside*
Nuclear Fuels      ● Drigg

Ramsey ●          ● Muncas
                        Mill
**ISLE OF MAN RAILWAYS**        Ravenglass ●
**(MANX ELECTRIC RAILWAY)**
**(3'0" Derby Castle -Ramsey)**   Bellevue ● ● Lewaigue
**(3'6" Laxey - Snaefell)**       Dreemskerry ●
                                  Ballajora ●          *Vickers*
                          Ballaglass ● Cornaa           *Gun*
                                  Glen Mona       Eskmeals    *Range*
                    Snaefell ● Dhoon Quarry                *Sidings*
                    (1990 ft)    Dhoon Glen
            Bungalow ●
                                                      ● Bootle
                    Depot
                    Laxey ● ● Minorca
            Fairy Cottage ● South Cape
            Ballabeg ●
            Garwick Glen ●
            Baldrine ●              *GROUDLE*
    Halfway (Baldromma) ●           *GLEN*
*ISLE*                 Lhen Sea Lion Rocks  *RAILWAY*
*OF MAN*               Coan ● Headland      *(2'0")*
                       Limekiln Halt
            Depots
**DOUGLAS CORP. HORSE TRAMS**  Derby Castle ● Groudle Glen
**(3'0" Pier - Derby Castle)**  Howstrake
            Douglas ● Onchan Head
                                    *TO HEYSHAM*
                Port         Douglas
                Soderick     Pier
**ISLE OF MAN RAILWAYS**  Santon              *TO FLEETWOOD*
**(STEAM OPERATED)**      (Loop
**(3'0")**                Disused)
    Colby (Loop
    (Disused)    Ballabeg
Port Erin ●    ● ● ● Ballasalla
        Port St. Mary  Castletown
                                *TO LIVERPOOL*
(All Ships Isle of Man Steam Packet Seaways)    *TO DUBLIN*

1                          2

0        5              10 m.
                           (1:350,0
0      5      10      15   km.

Aspatria

Baron Wood No. 2 Tun.
Baron Wood No. 1 Tun.

Lazonby &
Kirkoswald

*Lazonby Tun.*

Langwathby

*Culgaith
Tunnel*

Penrith

*Waste Bank
Tun.*

Newbiggin British
Gypsum Wks.

Keswick
Landing
Stage

**DERWENT
WATER**

Hawse End
Low Brandelhow
High Brandelhow

Ashness Gate
Lodore

*(Keswick
Launch)*

Pooley Bridge

**ULLSWATER**

*(Ullswater
Navigation &
Transit Co.)*

Howtown

Harrison's
Sidings – ARC

Glenridding

BSC Hardendale
Quarry

*CUMBRIA*

*Shap Summit
(916 ft)*

Ambleside

Beckfoot
Eskdale
(Dalegarth)
Irton
Road
Fisherground
The Green
*Black
Bridge*

*RAVENGLASS & ESKDALE
RAILWAY (1'3")*

Coniston

*(National
Trust)*

Brantwood
**CONISTON**

Park-a-Moor

Windermere
Staveley

Far
Sawrey
Bowness
Bowness

Burneside

Kendal

**WINDERMERE**

Oxenholme
Lake District

*(Windermere Iron
Steamboat Company)*

CE
Sidings

*Carnforth
East
Junc.*

CE
Shed

*Carnforth
F. & M.
Junc.*

R.O. Hodgson

Carnforth Stn.
Carnforth Junc.

Steam-
town

(1 : 90,000)

*LAKESIDE & HAVERTHWAITE
RAILWAY*

Lakeside
Newby Bridge

Haverthwaite

Foxfield

Green Road

Silecroft

Kirkby-in-
Furness

Millom

Askam

*Plumpton Junc.*
Fuel Services

Ulverston

Glaxochem
Works.

*Leven
Viaduct*

Grange-over-
Sands

Cark &
Cartmel

Kents
Bank

*Kent
Viaduct*

Arnside

Silverdale

*LANCS.*

*Park South Junc.*

*Lindal Tun.*

Dalton
*Dalton Tun.*
*Dalton Junc.*

*Melling
Tun.*

Carnforth

*(SEE INSET ABOVE)*

1

5
10 m.

(1:350,000)

5   10   15   km.

2

**66**

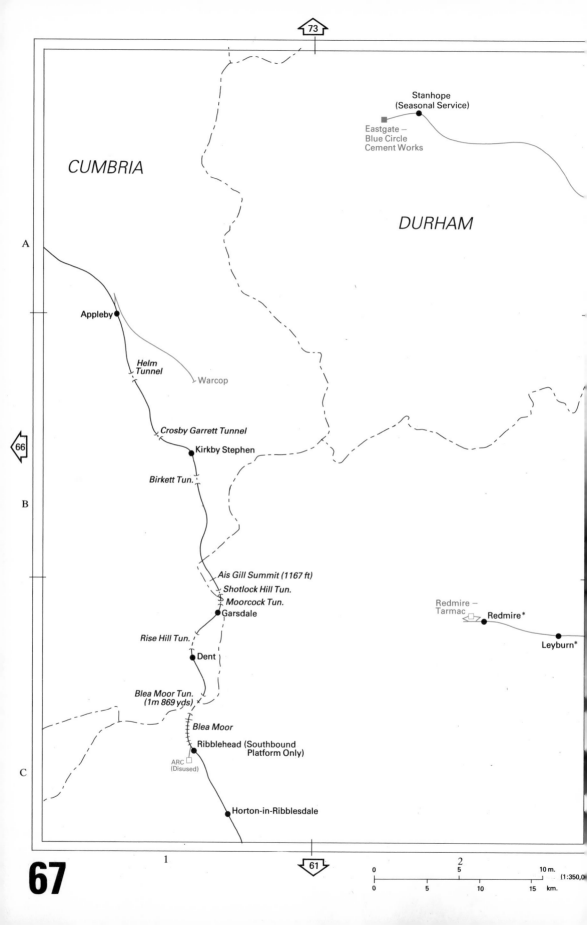

Stanhope
(Seasonal Service)

Eastgate –
Blue Circle
Cement Works

CUMBRIA

DURHAM

A

Appleby

Helm
Tunnel

Warcop

Crosby Garrett Tunnel

66

Kirkby Stephen

Birkett Tun.

B

Ais Gill Summit (1167 ft)

Shotlock Hill Tun.

Moorcock Tun.

Garsdale

Redmire –
Tarmac

Redmire*

Leyburn*

Rise Hill Tun.

Dent

Blea Moor Tun.
(1m 869 yds)

Blea Moor

Ribblehead (Southbound
Platform Only)

ARC
(Disused)

C

Horton-in-Ribblesdale

1

2
5

10 m.

(1:350,0

0

5

10

15

km.

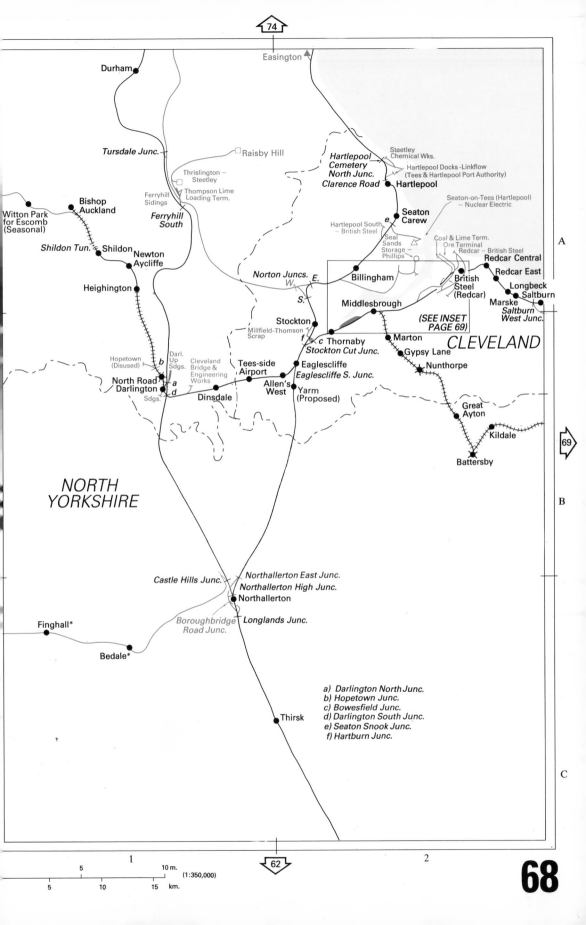

Durham

Easington

Tursdale Junc.

Raisby Hill

*Hartlepool*
*Cemetery*
*North Junc.*
*Clarence Road*

Steetley
Chemical Wks.

Hartlepool Docks -Linkflow
(Tees & Hartlepool Port Authority)

Hartlepool

Thrislington –
Steetley

Ferryhill
Sidings

Thompson Lime
Loading Term.

*Ferryhill*
*South*

Bishop
Auckland

Witton Park
for Escomb
(Seasonal)

Seaton
Carew

*e*

Seaton-on-Tees (Hartlepool)
– Nuclear Electric

Hartlepool South
– British Steel

*Shildon Tun.* Shildon Newton
Aycliffe

Seal
Sands
Storage –
Phillips

Coal & Lime Term.
Ore Terminal
Redcar – British Steel

A

Billingham

*Norton Juncs.* E.

Redcar Central

Redcar East

Heighington

W.

British
Steel
(Redcar)

Longbeck
Saltburn

S.

Middlesbrough

Marske

Saltburn
West Junc.

Stockton

Millfield–Thomson
Scrap

*(SEE INSET
PAGE 69)*

CLEVELAND

*f* *c* Thornaby
*Stockton Cut Junc.*

Marton

*Hopetown
(Disused)*

*b*

Darl.
Up
Sdgs.

Cleveland
Bridge &
Engineering
Works

North Road
Darlington

*a*
*d*

Sdgs.

Tees-side
Airport

Eaglescliffe

*Eaglescliffe S. Junc.*

Gypsy Lane

Nunthorpe

Allen's
West

Yarm
(Proposed)

Dinsdale

*Great
Ayton*

Kildale

69

NORTH
YORKSHIRE

Battersby

B

Castle Hills Junc.

*Northallerton East Junc.*
**Northallerton High Junc.**
Northallerton

Finghall*

*Boroughbridge
Road Junc.*

*Longlands Junc.*

Bedale*

a) Darlington North Junc.
b) Hopetown Junc.
c) Bowesfield Junc.
d) Darlington South Junc.
e) Seaton Snook Junc.
f) Hartburn Junc.

Thirsk

C

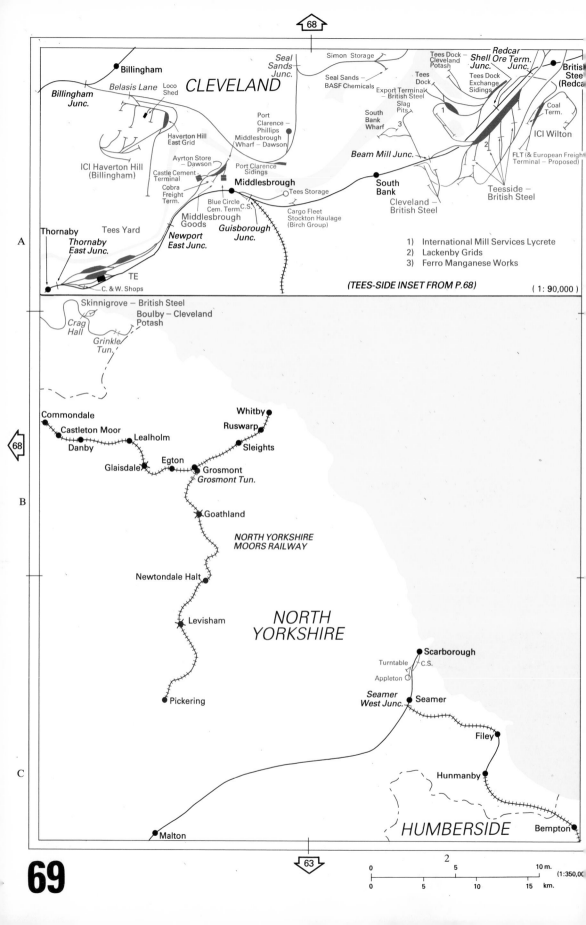

*Seal Sands Junc.*

Simon Storage

*Redcar Ore Term. Junc.*

Tees Dock – Shell Junc.

**CLEVELAND**

**Billingham**

*Billingham Junc.*

*Belasis Lane*

Loco Shed

Seal Sands – BASF Chemicals

Export Terminal – British Steel

Tees Dock

Tees Dock – Cleveland Potash

Tees Dock Exchange Sidings

Briti Steel (Redca

Haverton Hill East Grid

Port Clarence – Phillips

Middlesbrough Wharf – Dawson

Slag Pits

South Bank Wharf

Coal Term.

ICI Wilton

**ICI Haverton Hill**
**(Billingham)**

Ayrton Store – Dawson

Castle Cement Terminal

Cobra Freight Term.

Port Clarence Sidings

*Beam Mill Junc.*

FLT (& European Freigh Terminal – Proposed)

**Middlesbrough**

Tees Storage

**South Bank**

*Teesside – British Steel*

Blue Circle Cem. Term.

C.S.

**Thornaby**

Tees Yard

**Middlesbrough Goods**

*Newport East Junc.*

*Guisborough Junc.*

Cargo Fleet Stockton Haulage (Birch Group)

*Cleveland – British Steel*

*Thornaby East Junc.*

**A**

TE

C. & W. Shops

1) International Mill Services Lycrete
2) Lackenby Grids
3) Ferro Manganese Works

**(TEES-SIDE INSET FROM P.68)**

( 1: 90,000 )

Skinnigrove – British Steel

Boulby – Cleveland Potash

*Crag Hall*

*Grinkle Tun.*

**Commondale**

**Castleton Moor**

**Danby**

**Lealholm**

**Whitby**

**Ruswarp**

**Sleights**

**Glaisdale**

**Egton**

**Grosmont**
*Grosmont Tun.*

**B**

**Goathland**

*NORTH YORKSHIRE*
*MOORS RAILWAY*

**Newtondale Halt**

*NORTH*
*YORKSHIRE*

**Levisham**

**Scarborough**

Turntable

C.S.

Appleton

*Seamer West Junc.*

**Seamer**

**Pickering**

**Filey**

**C**

**Hunmanby**

**Malton**

*HUMBERSIDE*

**Bempton**

2

0     5     10 m.

(1:350,00

0     5     10     15 km.

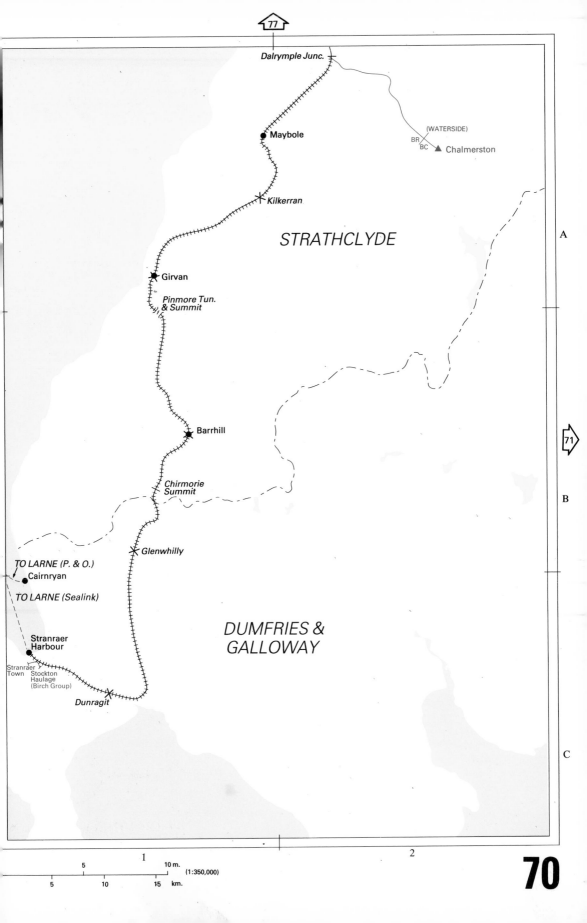

Dalrymple Junc.

(WATERSIDE)
BR
BC ▲ Chalmerston

● Maybole

✕ *Kilkerran*

*STRATHCLYDE*

A

★ Girvan

*Pinmore Tun.
& Summit*

★ Barrhill

71

*Chirmorie
Summit*

B

✕ *Glenwhilly*

*TO LARNE (P. & O.)*
● Cairnryan

*TO LARNE (Sealink)*

**Stranraer
Harbour**

*DUMFRIES &
GALLOWAY*

Stranraer
Town    Stockton
Haulage
(Birch Group)
● 

✕
*Dunragit*

C

Polquhap Summit

New Cumnock

*Bank Junc.*

Knockshinnoch

Kirkconnel

Beattock Summit (1015ft)

*STRATHCLYDE*

Drumlanrig Tunnel

A

*DUMFRIES & GALLOWAY*

Brunthill - MoD

Distribution Depot – Whittals Warehousing

Carlisle Kingmoor Yard

70

Stainton CE Tip (Disused)

Kingmoor Depot (Disused)

Maxwelltown – Scottish Oils

**Dumfries**

Maxwelltown – ICI Dumfries

Sidings

B

*CUMBRIA*

CARLISLE

Railcar Services

Carlisle London Rd. Goods

London Road Coal Depot – British Fuels (Disused)

**Carlisle**

Kemira Depot (Watt)

Sidings

*London Road Junc.*

*Bog Junc.*

*Upperby Junc.*

Petteril Bridge – Esso

Sidings

*Currock Junc.*

Currock C. & W. Shops

Upperby Carriage Depot (CL)

*Petteril Bridge Junc.*

Upperby Blue Circle Cem. Term.

*Upperby Bridge Junc.*

*(CARLISLE INSET FROM P.72)*

(1 : 70,000)

C

71

1

65

2

0        5        10 m.

(1:350,00

0    5    10    15    km.

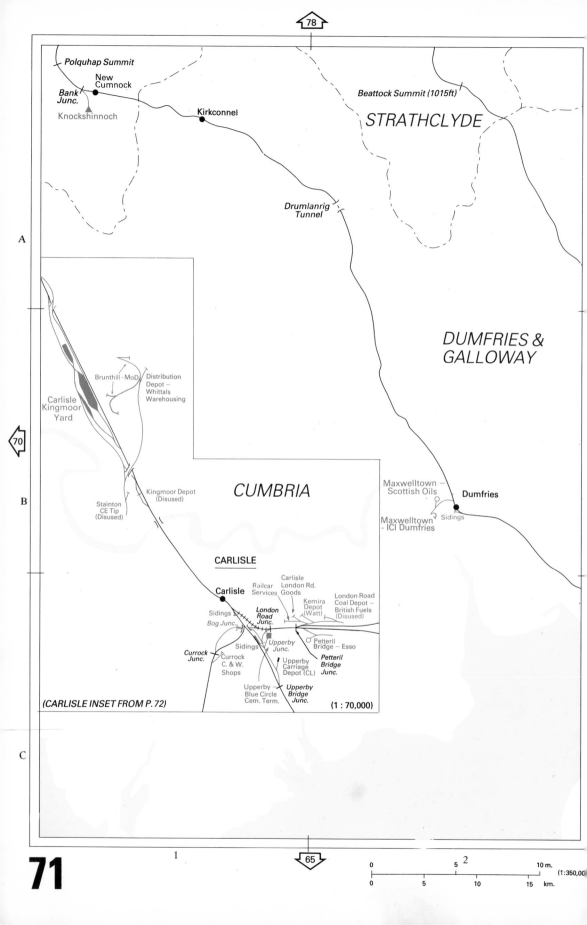

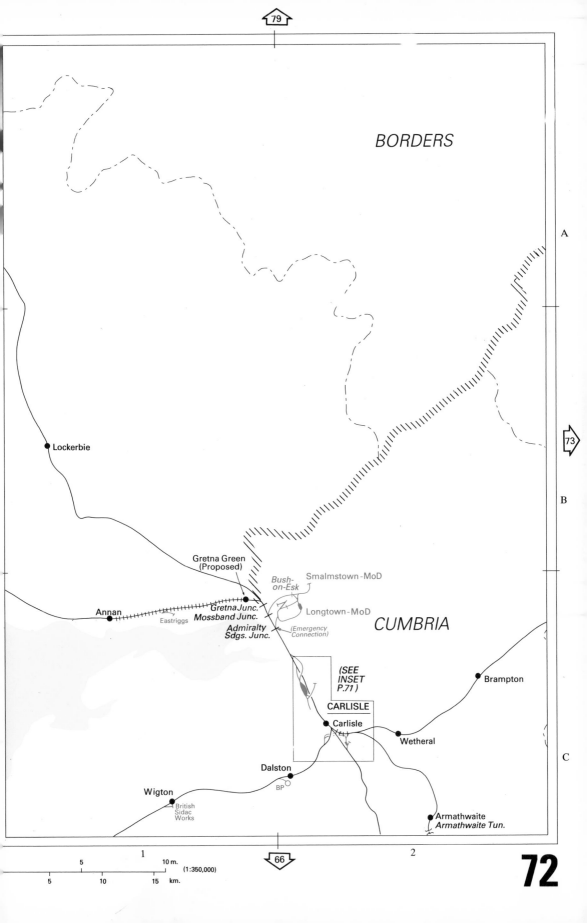

BORDERS

Lockerbie

Gretna Green
(Proposed)

Bush-
on-Esk

Smalmstown-MoD

Annan

Eastriggs

Gretna Junc.
Mossband Junc.

Longtown-MoD

CUMBRIA

Admiralty
Sdgs. Junc.

(Emergency
Connection)

(SEE
INSET
P.71)

Brampton

CARLISLE

Carlisle

Wetheral

Dalston

BP

Wigton

British
Sidac
Works

Armathwaite
Armathwaite Tun.

73

A

B

C

1

5

10 m.

(1:350,000)

5          10          15    km.

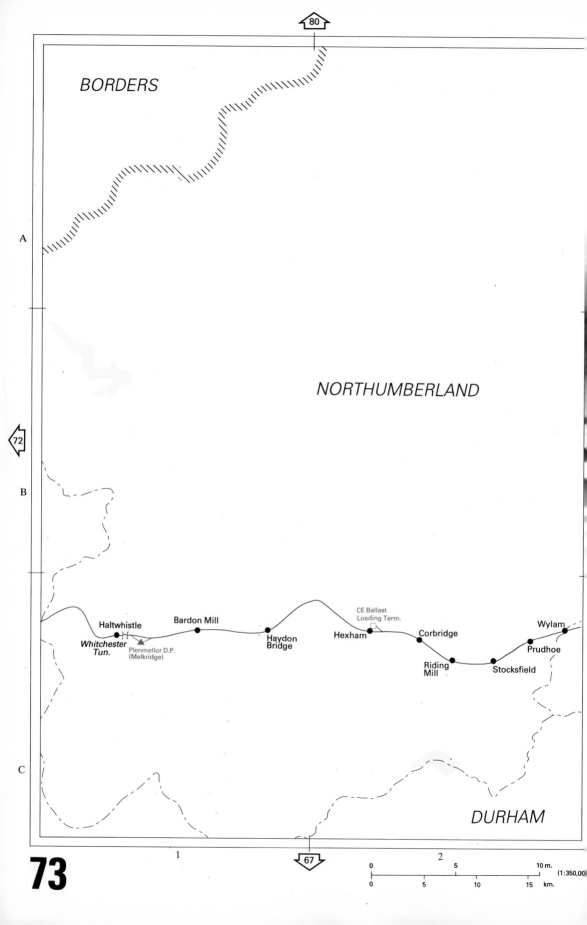

BORDERS

NORTHUMBERLAND

A

72

B

Haltwhistle   Bardon Mill                                                                        Wylam

*Whitchester*                                                                    Corbridge
*Tun.*          Plenmellor D.P.          Haydon          Hexham                              Prudhoe
                (Melkridge)              Bridge      CE Ballast
                                                     Loading Term.        Riding          Stocksfield
                                                                          Mill

C

DURHAM

**73**

1                              2

67

0          5                    10 m.
                                                              (1:350,00

0        5         10        15    km.

80

Alnmouth

Acklington

▲Widdrington

Widdrington

Butterwell ▲
*Butterwell*
*Junc.*

Alcan
Alum.
Wks.

Lynemouth
▲
*Alcan*
*Junc.*

Pegswood

*Ashington*

*Morpeth N. Junc.*
*Morpeth Junc.* Hepscott
Morpeth Junc.

*West*
*Sleekburn*
*Junc.*

*Marchey's House Junc.*
*Winning Junc.*

Blyth (Cambois) – National Power
BL

Sidings
& OLE
Depot

(Projected
curve)

*Bedlington*
*Junc.*
Bedlington
Furnaceway
Sidings

*Blyth Alcan*
Import Term.

Bates Staithes –
British Coal Terminal

*Newsham Junc.*

Cramlington

A

B

*TYNE*
*& WEAR*

Whitley Bay

Benton

Newcastle
Airport

South
Gosforth

Tynemouth

South
Shields

St. James

Newcastle

Blaydon

Heworth

*(SEE MAP 75)* Tyne
Yard

*(SEE MAP 76)*

Sunderland

*Ryhope Grange Junc.*
Ryhope Grange Sidings

Railway
Tramway

*BEAMISH MUSEUM*
*& TRAMWAY*

Chester-le-Street

Rye Hill (Possible
Opencast coal term.)

Seaham

Seaham
Seaham Dock & Harbour Co.
*Seabanks*

*(Disused)*

*Dawdon*
Locoshed
– BC

Pespool Tip

Murton
(To close)

C

5
1
10 m.

*(1:350,000)*

5
10
15 km.

2

**74**

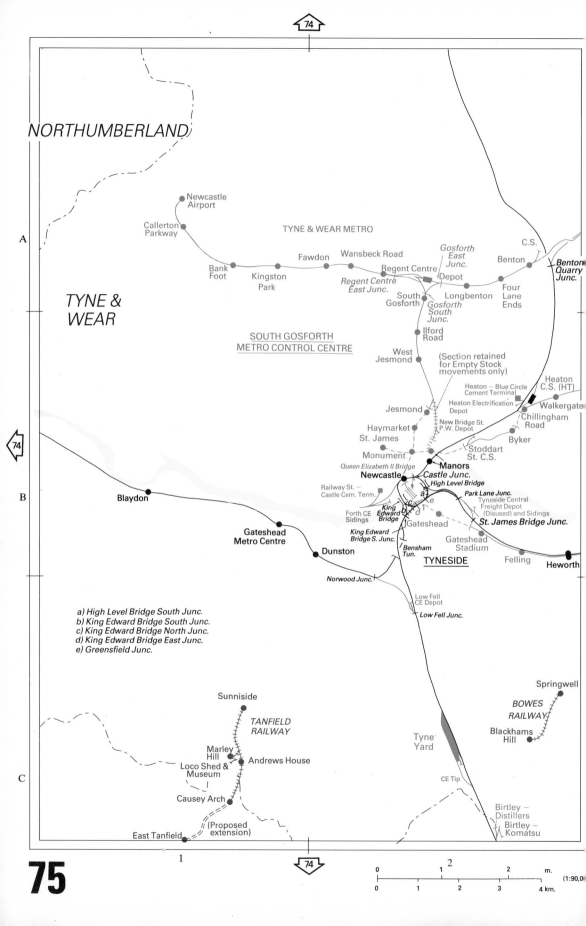

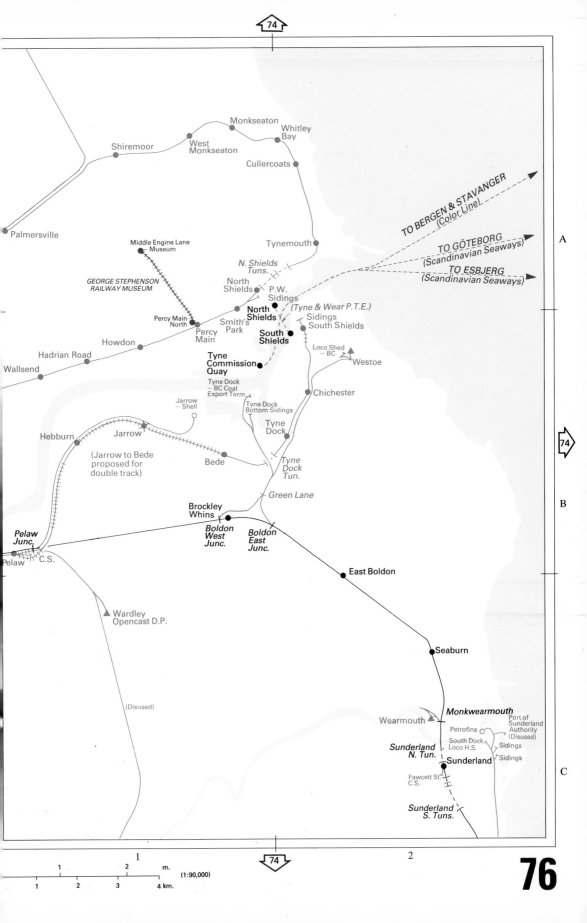

Shiremoor

West Monkseaton

Monkseaton

Whitley Bay

Palmersville

Cullercoats

TO BERGEN & STAVANGER (Color Line)

TO GÖTEBORG (Scandinavian Seaways)

TO ESBJERG (Scandinavian Seaways)

Tynemouth

Middle Engine Lane – Museum

GEORGE STEPHENSON RAILWAY MUSEUM

N. Shields Tuns.

North Shields

P.W. Sidings

(Tyne & Wear P.T.E.)

North Shields

Sidings

Percy Main North

Smith's Park

South Shields

South Shields

Percy Main

Hadrian Road

Howdon

Loco Shed – BC

Westoe

Wallsend

Tyne Commission Quay

Tyne Dock – BC Coal Export Term.

Chichester

Jarrow – Shell

Tyne Dock Bottom Sidings

Hebburn

Jarrow

(Jarrow to Bede proposed for double track)

Bede

Tyne Dock

Tyne Dock Tun.

Green Lane

Brockley Whins

Pelaw Junc.

Boldon West Junc.

Boldon East Junc.

Pelaw

C.S.

East Boldon

Wardley Opencast D.P.

(Disused)

Seaburn

Monkwearmouth

Wearmouth

Port of Sunderland Authority (Disused)

Petrofina

South Dock Loco H.S.

Sidings

Sidings

Sunderland N. Tun.

Sunderland

Fawcett St. C.S.

Sunderland S. Tuns.

1

2

m.

1    2

1    2    3    4 km.

(1:90,000)

**76**

Garelochhead

Luss

*(Loch Lomond
Marina Co.)*

LOCH
LOMOND

Helensburgh
Upper

Helensburgh Central
Kilcreggan

Craigendoran
*Craigendoran
Junc.*

Balloch Pier
Balloch

Alexandria

*(Cal-Mac)*
*(Western Ferries)*
Gourock

*(Clyde
Marine)*
Fort
Matilda

Cardross

Renton

Hunter's
Quay

Greenock West
Greenock Central
Cartsdyke

*Dalreoch
Tuns.*

Dunoon

*(Cal-Mac)*
IBM *
Halt

Bogston
c

Dalreoch

Dumbarton Cen.
Dumbarton East

*(SEE MAP 81)*

Milngavie

McInroy's
Point

e

*James Watt Dock
(Disused)*
Woodhall

*No.2
Tun.*

Bowling

COWAL

Branchton
Whinhill

d
b
Port
Glasgow

Langbank
British Aerospace

*Bishopton
No.1 Tun.*

Dalmuir

Singer

*Dunrod*

Inverkip
*Inverkip
Tun.*

Bishopton

Yoker

Wemyss
Bay

a) Ladyburn Junc.
b) Wemyss Bay Junc.
c) Newton St. Tun.
  (1m 351yds )
  (Temporarily single line)
d) Cartsburn Tun.
e) Ann St. Tun.
f) Wellpark Tun.

Paisley
Gilmour
St.

Rothesay

ISLE OF
BUTE

Johnstone
Milliken Park

Paisley
Canal

**A**

Barrhead

Neilston

Cumbrae
Slip

Largs

Lochwinnoch

ISLE OF
GT. CUMBRAE
Millport

MoD
*Fairlie
Tun.*

Lugton – Kemira
Fertiliser Depot

*(Cal-Mac)*

Fairlie
Fairlie High –
Scottish
Nuclear

*Distribution
Depot – Young
(Disused)*

Glengarnock
Giffen

*Lugton*

Hunterston
BSC Ore
Reduction
Plant
(Disused)

Hunterston
Ore Terminal

West
Kilbride

*Dalry –
Roche
Products*

*(Disused)*

Dunlop

*Swinlees*
Dalry

Stewarton

**B**

*Holm
Junc.*

Ardrossan
South Beach

Sdgs.

Kilwinning

Ardrossan
Harbour

*Dubbs
Junc.*

*Byrehill Junc.*

*STRATHCLYDE*

*(Cal-Mac)*
TO BRODICK (ARRAN)

Ardrossan
Town

Saltcoats

ICI Snodgrass
ICI
Ardeer

*Bogside Junc.*

Kilmaurs

J. Walker Distillery

Stevenston
Irvine
CE Depot

Blue Circle
Cement Term.
CE Works
Caberboard

CE Sidings

Kilmarnock
Kay Park Junc.

Riccarton
– BP

Barleith – J. Walker
Distillery

*Irvine –
Caledonian Paper*

Shewalton
CE Tip

Locomotive Works
Hunslet – Barclay (KK)

*Falkland Junc.*

*Meadowhead*

Falkland
Yard

Newton-
on-Ayr

*Barassie Junc.*

*Ayr Harbour Junc.*
SAI Works

Barassie

*Newton
Junc.*

Troon
Barassie
CE Sidings

*(Reversing Spur)*

*Mossgiel
Tun.*

Ayr Harbour
& Coal
Terminal

AY

Prestwick – BP

*Mauchline Junc.*

Prestwick

*Annbank Junc.*

**C**

Ayr

Townhead C.S.

Heathfield (Projected)
Newton-
on-Ayr

Auchincruive
– Esso

(1 : 90,000)

*(AYR INSET
FROM RIGHT)*

Ayr

*(SEE INSET
TO LEFT)*

Auchinleck

Killoch
Washery

1

2

0       5       10 m.

(1:350,0

0    5    10    15   km.

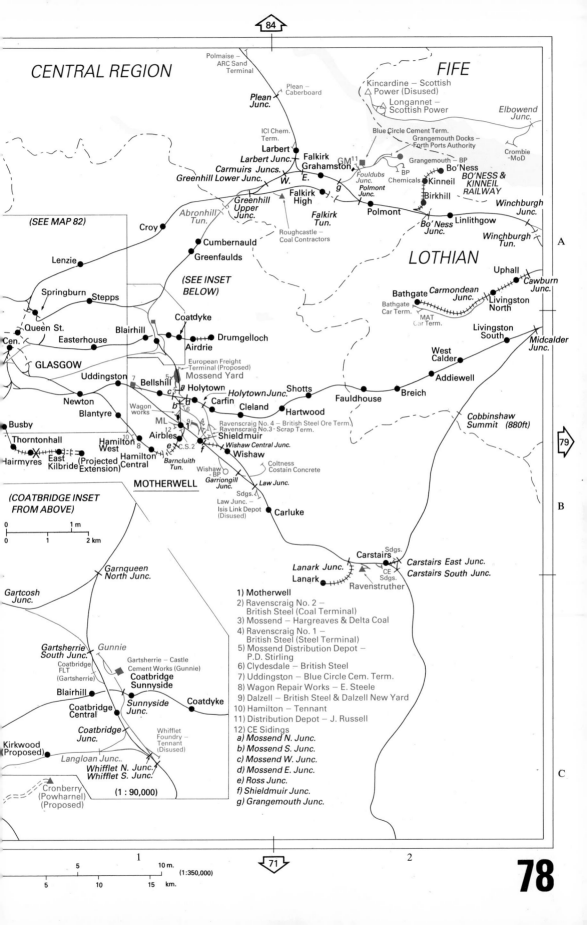

CENTRAL REGION

FIFE

LOTHIAN

*(SEE MAP 82)*

*(SEE INSET BELOW)*

GLASSGOW

*(COATBRIDGE INSET FROM ABOVE)*

MOTHERWELL

**BO'NESS & KINNEIL RAILWAY**

Polmaise – ARC Sand Terminal
Plean – Caberboard
Kincardine – Scottish Power (Disused)
Longannet – Scottish Power
Elbowend Junc.
Blue Circle Cement Term.
Grangemouth Docks – Forth Ports Authority
ICI Chem. Term.
GM 11
Grangemouth – BP
Crombie –MoD
Larbert
Larbert Junc.
Falkirk
Fouldubs Junc.
BP Chemicals
Bo'Ness
*Carmuirs Juncs.*
Grahamston
Kinneil
*Greenhill Lower Junc.*
W.  E.
g
Polmont Junc.
Birkhill
Greenhill Upper Junc.
Falkirk High
Polmont
Bo'Ness Junc.
Linlithgow
Winchburgh Junc.
*Abronhill Tun.*
Falkirk Tun.
Croy
Roughcastle – Coal Contractors
Winchburgh Tun.
A
Cumbernauld
Greenfaulds
Uphall
Cawburn Junc.
Lenzie
Bathgate
*Carmondean Junc.*
Livingston North
Springburn
Stepps
Bathgate Car Term.
MAT Car Term.
Livingston South
Queen St.
Coatdyke
Midcalder Junc.
Cen.
Blairhill
Easterhouse
Drumgelloch
Airdrie
West Calder
Uddingston
Bellshill
European Freight Terminal (Proposed)
Mossend Yard
Addiewell
Breich
Newton
c
a
Holytown
Holytown Junc.
Shotts
Fauldhouse
Blantyre
Wagon works
b
d
Carfin
Cleland
Hartwood
79
Busby
ML
Ravenscraig No. 4 – British Steel Ore Term.
*Cobbinshaw Summit (880ft)*
Thorntonhall
Airbles
Ravenscraig No.3– Scrap Term.
Hamilton West
e
C.S.2
Shieldmuir
*Wishaw Central Junc.*
Hairmyres
East Kilbride
*(Projected Extension)*
Hamilton Central
*Barncluith Tun.*
Wishaw
Coltness Costain Concrete
Wishaw – BP
*Garriongill Junc.*
Law Junc.
B
Sdgs.
Law Junc. – Isis Link Depot (Disused)
Carluke

*(COATBRIDGE INSET FROM ABOVE)*

0     1 m
0        1        2 km

Garnqueen North Junc.
Lanark Junc.
Carstairs
Sdgs.
Carstairs East Junc.
Gartcosh Junc.
Lanark
CE Sdgs.
Carstairs South Junc.
Ravenstruther

Gartsherrie South Junc.
*Gunnie*
Coatbridge FLT (Gartsherrie)
Gartsherrie – Castle Cement Works (Gunnie)
Coatbridge Sunnyside
Blairhill
Sunnyside Junc.
Coatdyke
Coatbridge Central
*Coatbridge Junc.*
Whifflet Foundry – Tennant (Disused)
Kirkwood (Proposed)
*Langloan Junc.*
*Whifflet N. Junc.*
*Whifflet S. Junc.*
(1 : 90,000)
Cronberry (Powharnel) (Proposed)

1) Motherwell
2) Ravenscraig No. 2 – British Steel (Coal Terminal)
3) Mossend – Hargreaves & Delta Coal
4) Ravenscraig No. 1 – British Steel (Steel Terminal)
5) Mossend Distribution Depot – P.D. Stirling
6) Clydesdale – British Steel
7) Uddingston – Blue Circle Cem. Term.
8) Wagon Repair Works – E. Steele
9) Dalzell – British Steel & Dalzell New Yard
10) Hamilton – Tennant
11) Distribution Depot – J. Russell
12) CE Sidings
a) Mossend N. Junc.
b) Mossend S. Junc.
c) Mossend W. Junc.
d) Mossend E. Junc.
e) Ross Junc.
f) Shieldmuir Junc.
g) Grangemouth Junc.

1        10 m.
5              (1:350,000)
5        10        15   km.

84
71
79

**78**

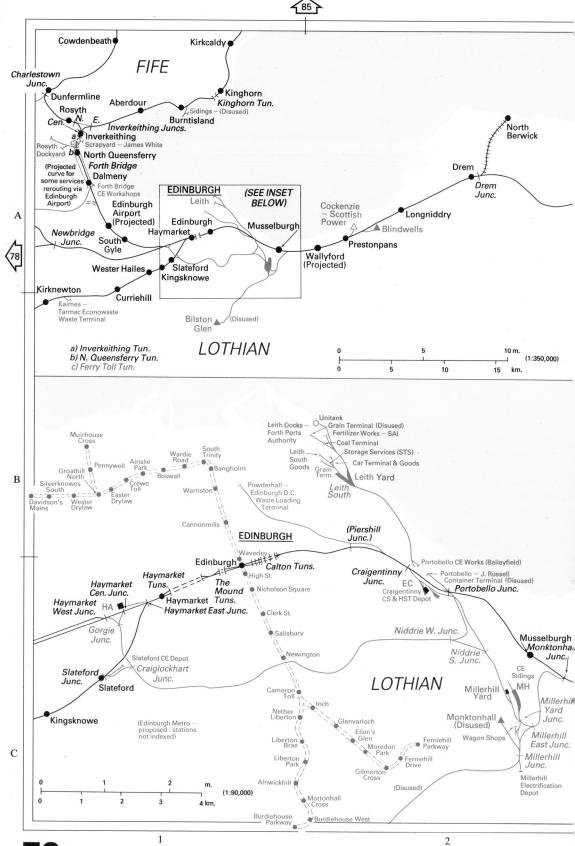

78

**FIFE**

Cowdenbeath
Kirkcaldy

*Charlestown Junc.*
Dunfermline
Aberdour
Kinghorn
*Kinghorn Tun.*
Rosyth *Cen.*
*N. E.*
Burntisland
Sidings – (Disused)
*Inverkeithing Juncs.*
*a* Inverkeithing
Scrapyard – James White
Rosyth Dockyard
*b* North Queensferry
*Forth Bridge*
Dalmeny
Forth Bridge CE Workshops
(Projected curve for some services rerouting via Edinburgh Airport)

North Berwick
Drem
*Drem Junc.*

**EDINBURGH**
Leith
*(SEE INSET BELOW)*

Edinburgh Airport (Projected)
Edinburgh
Haymarket
Musselburgh
Cockenzie – Scottish Power
Blindwells
Longniddry
Prestonpans
Wallyford (Projected)

A

*Newbridge Junc.*
South Gyle
Wester Hailes
Slateford
Kingsknowe

Kirknewton
Kaimes – Tarmac Econowaste Waste Terminal
Curriehill

Bilston Glen (Disused)

*a) Inverkeithing Tun.*
*b) N. Queensferry Tun.*
*c) Ferry Toll Tun.*

**LOTHIAN**

| 0 | | 5 | | 10 m. |
|---|---|---|---|---|
| | | | | (1:350,000) |
| 0 | 5 | 10 | 15 | km. |

B

Muirhouse Cross
Groathill North
Pennywell
Ainslie Park
Wardie Road
South Trinity
Silverknowes South
Crewe Toll
Boswall
Bangholm
Davidson's Mains
Wester Drylaw
Easter Drylaw
Warriston
Cannonmills

Leith Docks – Forth Ports Authority
Unitank
Grain Terminal (Disused)
Fertilizer Works – SAI
Coal Terminal
Storage Services (STS)
Car Terminal & Goods
Leith South Goods
Grain Term.
Leith Yard
*Leith South*

Powderhall – Edinburgh D.C. Waste Loading Terminal

*(Piershill Junc.)*

**EDINBURGH**
Waverley
Edinburgh
*Calton Tuns.*
High St.
Nicholson Square
*Haymarket Tuns.*
*Haymarket Cen. Junc.*
HA
*The Mound Tuns.*
*Haymarket West Junc.*
Haymarket
*Haymarket East Junc.*
*Gorgie Junc.*
Clerk St.
Salisbury
*Craigentinny Junc.*
EC
Craigentinny CS & HST Depot
Portobello CE Works (Baileyfield)
Portobello – J. Russell Container Terminal (Disused)
**Portobello Junc.**

Slateford CE Depot
*Craiglockhart Junc.*
*Slateford Junc.*
Slateford
Newington
*Niddrie W. Junc.*
*Niddrie S. Junc.*
Musselburgh
*Monktonha*
*Monktonha Junc.*
CE Sidings
MH

Kingsknowe
(Edinburgh Metro – proposed : stations not indexed)

Cameron Toll
Inch
Nether Liberton
Glenvarloch
Ellen's Glen
Moredun Park
Ferniehill Parkway
Ferniehill Drive
Millerhill Yard
Monktonhall (Disused)
Wagon Shops
*Millerhill Yard Junc.*
*Millerhill East Junc.*
*Millerhill Junc.*
**LOTHIAN**

Liberton Brae
Liberton Park
Gilmerton Cross
Alnwickhill
(Disused)
Millerhill Electrification Depot

C

| 0 | 1 | | 2 | m. |
|---|---|---|---|---|
| | | | | (1:90,000) |
| 0 | 1 | 2 | 3 | 4 km. |

Mortonhall Cross
Burdiehouse Parkway
Burdiehouse West

1
2

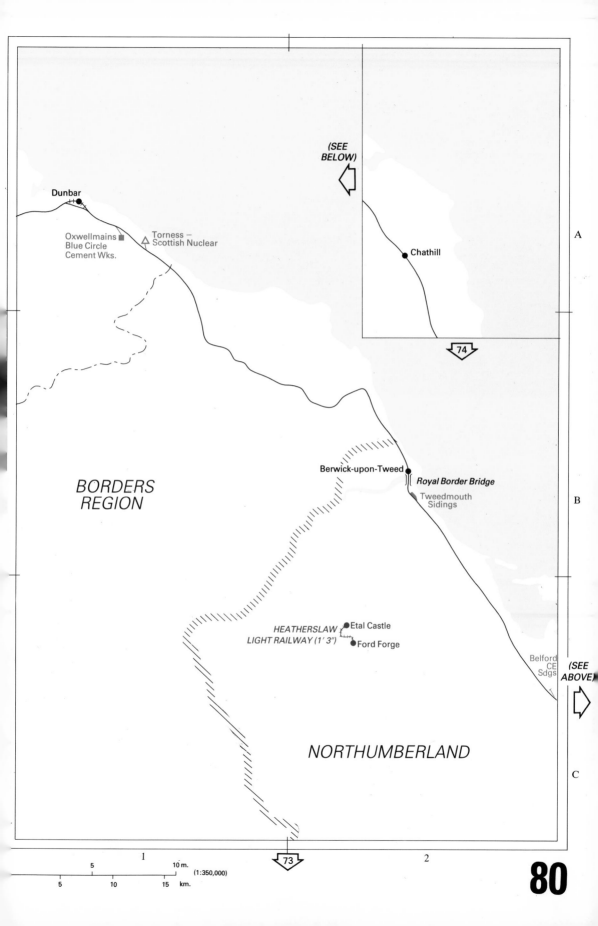

Dunbar

Oxwellmains
Blue Circle
Cement Wks.

Torness –
Scottish Nuclear

*(SEE
BELOW)*

Chathill

A

74

BORDERS
REGION

Berwick-upon-Tweed

*Royal Border Bridge*

Tweedmouth
Sidings

B

*HEATHERSLAW
LIGHT RAILWAY (1' 3")*

Etal Castle

Ford Forge

Belford
CE
Sdgs

*(SEE
ABOVE)*

NORTHUMBERLAND

C

1

5

10 m.

(1:350,000)

5

10

15

km.

73

2

**80**

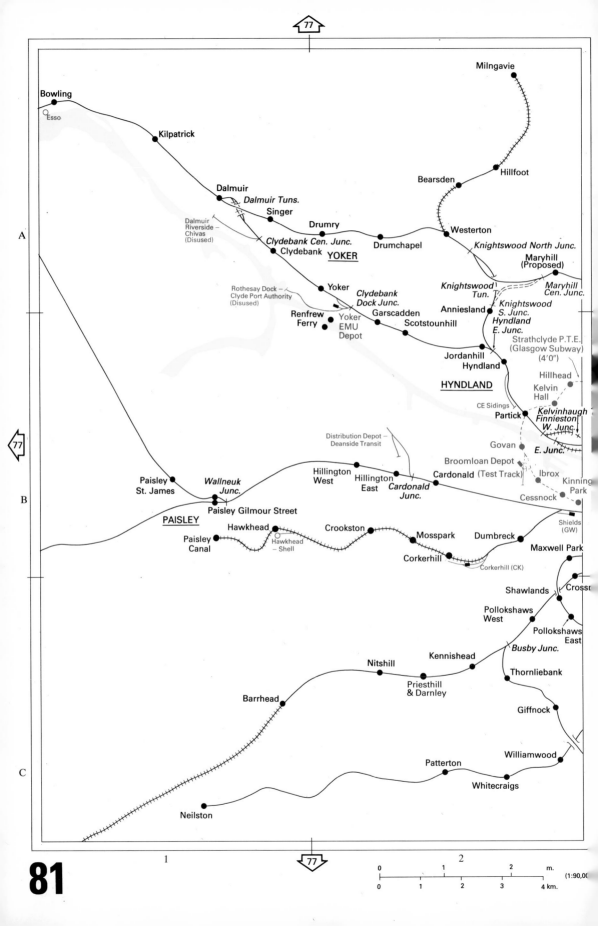

Milngavie

Bowling

Esso

Kilpatrick

Hillfoot

Bearsden

Westerton

Dalmuir

*Dalmuir Tuns.*

Singer

Drumry

*Knightswood North Junc.*

Dalmuir
Riverside –
Chivas
(Disused)

*Clydebank Cen. Junc.*
Clydebank

Drumchapel

**YOKER**

Maryhill
(Proposed)

A

Rothesay Dock –
Clyde Port Authority
(Disused)

Yoker

*Clydebank
Dock Junc.*

*Knightswood
Tun.*

*Maryhill
Cen. Junc.*

Garscadden

Anniesland

*Knightswood
S. Junc.*

Renfrew
Ferry

Yoker
EMU
Depot

Scotstounhill

*Hyndland
E. Junc.*

Jordanhill

Hyndland

Strathclyde P.T.E.
(Glasgow Subway)
(4'0")

Hillhead

Kelvin
Hall

**HYNDLAND**

CE Sidings

*Kelvinhaugh
Finnieston
W. Junc.*

Partick

Govan

Distribution Depot –
Deanside Transit

Broomloan Depot

*E. Junc.*

Hillington
West

Hillington
East

Cardonald (Test Track)

Ibrox

Kinning
Park

Cardonald
Junc.

Cessnock

Paisley
St. James

*Wallneuk
Junc.*

Shields
(GW)

B

Paisley Gilmour Street

**PAISLEY**

Hawkhead

Crookston

Mosspark

Dumbreck

Maxwell Park

Paisley
Canal

Hawkhead
– Shell

Corkerhill

Corkerhill (CK)

Crossr

Shawlands

Pollokshaws
West

Pollokshaws
East

Kennishead

*Busby Junc.*

Nitshill

Thornliebank

Priesthill
& Darnley

Giffnock

Barrhead

Williamwood

Patterton

Whitecraigs

C

Neilston

0          1          2          m.
(1:90,00

0      1      2      3      4 km.

**81**

# STRATHCLYDE

Lenzie

Bishopbriggs – Shell

Cadder CE Sidings

(Proposed Anniesland to Glasgow Queen St. new service)

Bishopbriggs

A

Stepps

Summerston (Proposed)

## COWLAIRS

*Cowlairs E. Junc.*  Eastfield (ED)

Cadder (Proposed)

*Cowlairs N. Junc.*
*Cowlairs W. Junc.*  Cowlairs C.S. (GC)
*Sighthill West Junc.*

Gartcosh Distribution Depot – J.G. Russell

78

*Cowlairs S. Junc.*  Springburn
*Sighthill Junc.*
**Barnhill**

Kelvinbridge

Scrapyard MC Metals

St. George's Cross

Buchanan St.

*Barnhill Tun.*

Cowcaddens

BRML Glasgow (ZH)

*Blochairn Tun.*

aring Cross

*Queen St. H.L. Tun.*

Glasgow Queen St.
*High St. Tun.*

Alexandra Parade

Easterhouse

j      h

High St.
*High St. Junc.*

Duke St.
*Duke St. Tun.*

Carntyne

Shettleston

Garrowhill

k
2

Glasgow Central  9      4

**GLAS. CEN.**  6

Bellgrove

CE Workshops

CE Sidings (To close)

B

Bargeddie (Proposed)

*Canning St. Tun.*

g

*Dalmarnock Rd. Tun.*

Baillieston (Proposed)

8   7   a

Bridgeton
*Eglinton St. Tuns.*

Gushetfaulds FLT
BOC (Disused)

London Rd. Scrapyard – Adam
London Road – N.E.I.
Dalmarnock Ironworks

Mount Vernon (Proposed)

ields unc.

n   m

Dalmarnock

5      e   f

d

c

Polmadie C.S. (PO & PC)

C.S.

*Rutherglen Juncs.*   N.
W.   11

*Strathclyde Junc.*

Bridgeton Yard – CE
Rutherglen CE Depot

CE Plant Depot

Carmyle (Proposed)

(Proposed reopening to passengers for Coatbridge Central to Glasgow service)

Crosshill

Rutherglen
*Cen.*

Uddingston

Queen's Park

Mount Florida

N. Cathcart Juncs.

*Rutherglen East Junc.*

Newton East Junc.

*Uddingston Junc.*

Langside

Cathcart
W.      E.

King's Park

Croftfoot

Cambuslang

Newton

Siding

## CATHCART

Burnside

Kirkhill
*Kirkhill Tun.*

Newton West Junc.

Blantyre

C

Muirend

Clarkston

1) Pollokshields East
2) Exhibition Centre
3) Anderston
4) Argyle Street
5) Pollokshields West
6) Bridge St.
7) West St.
8) Shields Rd.
9) St. Enoch
10) Muirhouse CE Workshops
11) Rutherglen Training Centre

a) Bridge St. Junc.
b) Eglinton St. Junc.
c) Larkfield Junc.
d) Muirhouse South Junc.
e) Muirhouse Central Junc.
f) Muirhouse North Junc.
g) Anderston Tun. (1m 1010yds.)
h) Charing Cross Tun.
j) Finnieston Tun.
k) Stobcross St. Tun.      m) West St. Tun.
l) Bellgrove Tuns.          n) Terminus Junc.

Busby

1

m.

(1:90,000)

1   2   3   4 km.

2

# 82

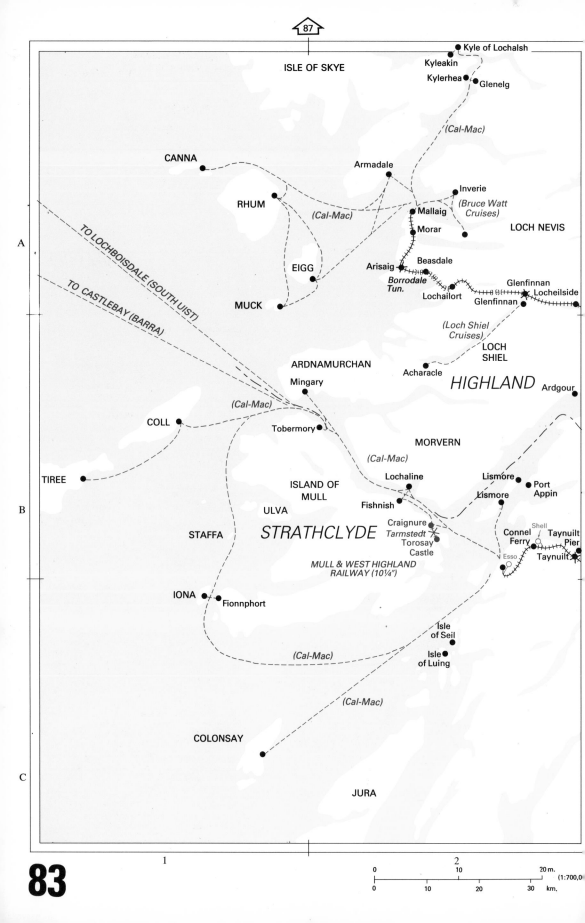

ISLE OF SKYE

Kyle of Lochalsh
Kyleakin
Kylerhea
Glenelg

*(Cal-Mac)*

CANNA

Armadale

Inverie

*(Bruce Watt Cruises)*

RHUM

*(Cal-Mac)*

Mallaig

Morar

LOCH NEVIS

A

EIGG

TO LOCHBOISDALE (SOUTH UIST)

TO CASTLEBAY (BARRA)

MUCK

Arisaig
*Borrodale Tun.*

Beasdale

Lochailort

Glenfinnan
Glenfinnan

Glenfinnan
Locheilside

*(Loch Shiel Cruises)*

ARDNAMURCHAN

Mingary

Acharacle

LOCH SHIEL

HIGHLAND

Ardgour

*(Cal-Mac)*

COLL

Tobermory

MORVERN

*(Cal-Mac)*

TIREE

ISLAND OF MULL

Lochaline

Lismore
Port Appin

B

ULVA

STAFFA

*STRATHCLYDE*

Fishnish

Lismore

Connel Ferry
Shell
Taynuilt Pier

Craignure
*Tarmstedt*
Torosay Castle

Esso

Taynuilt

*MULL & WEST HIGHLAND RAILWAY (10¼")*

IONA

Fionnphort

Isle of Seil

Isle of Luing

*(Cal-Mac)*

*(Cal-Mac)*

COLONSAY

C

JURA

0        10        20 m.
(1:700,0

0    10    20    30    km.

**83**

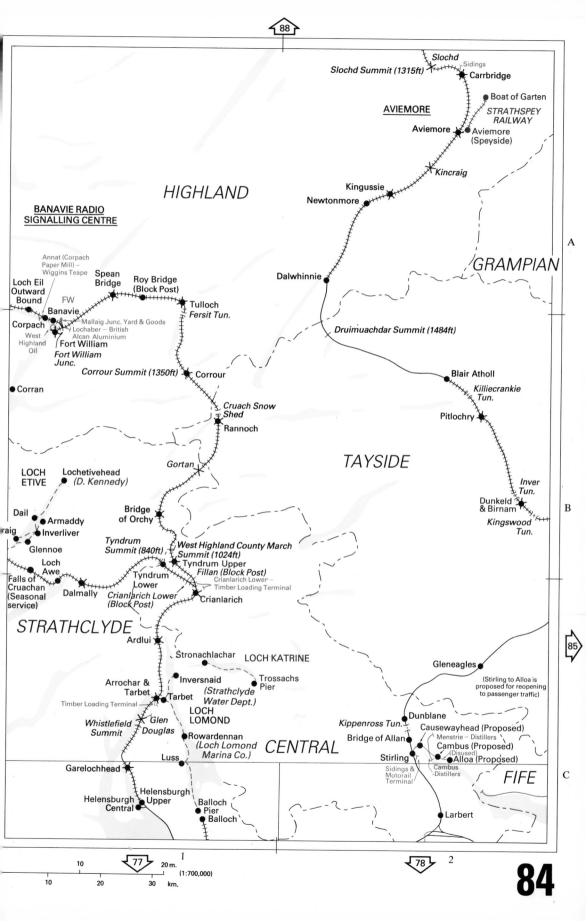

Slochd
Slochd Summit (1315ft)
Sidings
Carrbridge
Boat of Garten
STRATHSPEY RAILWAY
AVIEMORE
Aviemore
Aviemore (Speyside)
Kincraig
Kingussie
Newtonmore

HIGHLAND

GRAMPIAN

A

BANAVIE RADIO SIGNALLING CENTRE

Dalwhinnie

Annat (Corpach Paper Mill) — Wiggins Teape
Spean Bridge
Roy Bridge (Block Post)
Loch Eil Outward Bound
FW
Banavie
Tulloch
Fersit Tun.
Corpach
Mallaig Junc. Yard & Goods
Lochaber — British Alcan Aluminium
West Highland Oil
Fort William
Fort William Junc.

Druimuachdar Summit (1484ft)

Blair Atholl

Corrour Summit (1350ft)
Corrour
Killiecrankie Tun.
Corran
Pitlochry

Cruach Snow Shed
Rannoch

TAYSIDE

Gortan

LOCH ETIVE
Lochetivehead (D. Kennedy)

Inver Tun.

Dail
Armaddy
Inverliver
Bridge of Orchy
Dunkeld & Birnam
B
raig
Glennoe
Kingswood Tun.

Loch Awe
Tyndrum Summit (840ft)
West Highland County March Summit (1024ft)
Tyndrum Upper
Fillan (Block Post)
Falls of Cruachan (Seasonal service)
Tyndrum Lower
Crianlarich Lower — Timber Loading Terminal
Dalmally
Crianlarich Lower (Block Post)
Crianlarich

STRATHCLYDE

Ardlui

Stronachlachar
LOCH KATRINE
Gleneagles
(Stirling to Alloa is proposed for reopening to passenger traffic)

Inversnaid
Trossachs Pier

Arrochar & Tarbet
Tarbet
(Strathclyde Water Dept.)
85

Timber Loading Terminal
LOCH LOMOND
Dunblane
Kippenross Tun.
Causewayhead (Proposed)
Menstrie – Distillers
Whistlefield Summit
Glen Douglas
Rowardennan
(Loch Lomond Marina Co.)
Bridge of Allan
Cambus (Proposed)
(Disused)
Alloa (Proposed)
Luss
CENTRAL
Stirling
Cambus Distillers
Garelochhead
Sidings & Motorail Terminal
FIFE
C

Helensburgh Central
Helensburgh Upper
Balloch Pier
Balloch
Larbert

10
77
20 m.
(1:700,000)
1
78
2

10
20
30
km.

**84**

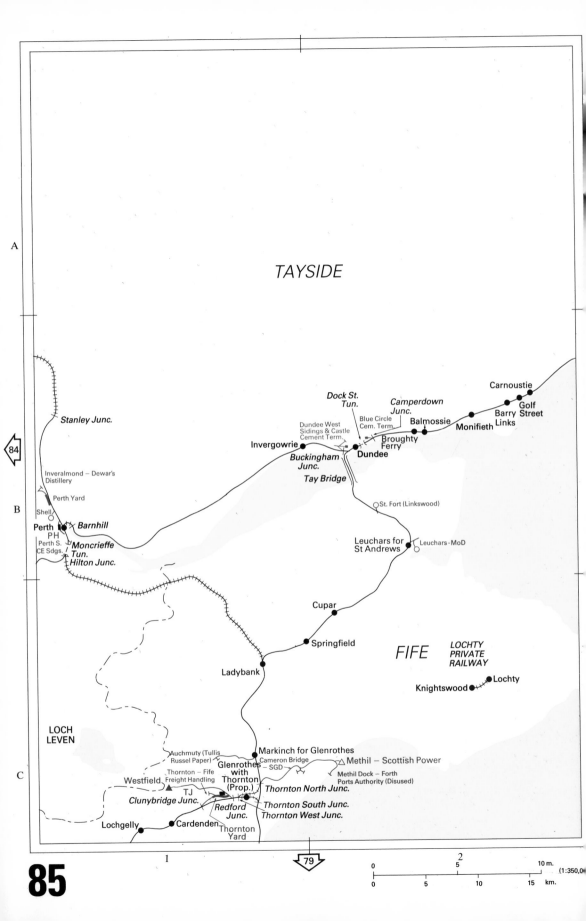

TAYSIDE

Carnoustie

Golf
Street

Barry
Links

Monifieth

Balmossie

*Camperdown
Junc.*

*Dock St.
Tun.*

Blue Circle
Cem. Term.

Broughty
Ferry

Dundee West
Sidings & Castle
Cement Term.

Invergowrie

*Buckingham
Junc.*

*Tay Bridge*

*Stanley Junc.*

St. Fort (Linkswood)

84

Inveralmond – Dewar's
Distillery

Perth Yard

Leuchars for
St Andrews

Leuchars-MoD

Shell

Perth
PH

*Barnhill*

B

Perth S.
CE Sdgs.

*Moncrieffe
Tun.
Hilton Junc.*

Cupar

Springfield

FIFE

LOCHTY
PRIVATE
RAILWAY

Ladybank

Knightswood

Lochty

LOCH
LEVEN

Auchmuty (Tullis
Russel Paper)

Markinch for Glenrothes

Cameron Bridge
– SGD

Methil – Scottish Power

Westfield

*Glenrothes
with
Thornton
(Prop.)*

Methil Dock – Forth
Ports Authority (Disused)

Thornton – Fife
Freight Handling

TJ

C

*Clunybridge Junc.*

*Thornton North Junc.*

*Redford
Junc.*

*Thornton South Junc.*
*Thornton West Junc.*

Lochgelly

Cardenden

Thornton
Yard

1

**85**

79

0        2        10 m.
         5
                  (1:350,0

0    5    10    15  km.

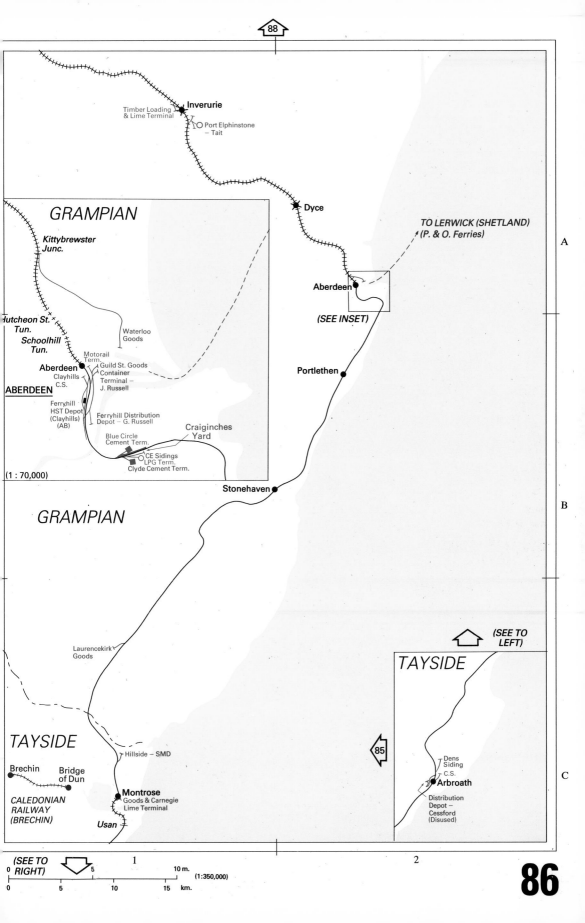

Inverurie

Timber Loading
& Lime Terminal

Port Elphinstone
– Tait

Dyce

TO LERWICK (SHETLAND)
(P. & O. Ferries)

A

Aberdeen

(SEE INSET)

*GRAMPIAN*

*Kittybrewster
Junc.*

Waterloo
Goods

*Hutcheon St.
Tun.*

*Schoolhill
Tun.*

**Aberdeen**

Motorail
Term.

Guild St. Goods

Container
Terminal –
J. Russell

**ABERDEEN**

Clayhills
C.S.

Ferryhill
HST Depot
(Clayhills)
(AB)

Ferryhill Distribution
Depot – G. Russell

Craiginches
Yard

Blue Circle
Cement Term.

CE Sidings
LPG Term.
Clyde Cement Term.

(1 : 70,000)

Portlethen

**Stonehaven**

*GRAMPIAN*

B

Laurencekirk
Goods

*(SEE TO
LEFT)*

*TAYSIDE*

*TAYSIDE*

85

Dens
Siding
C.S.

Hillside – SMD

**Arbroath**

C

Brechin     Bridge
            of Dun

Distribution
Depot –
Cessford
(Disused)

*CALEDONIAN
RAILWAY
(BRECHIN)*

**Montrose**
Goods & Carnegie
Lime Terminal

*Usan*

*(SEE TO
RIGHT)*

0        5        1

0   5      10      15    km.

10 m.

(1:350,000)

**86**

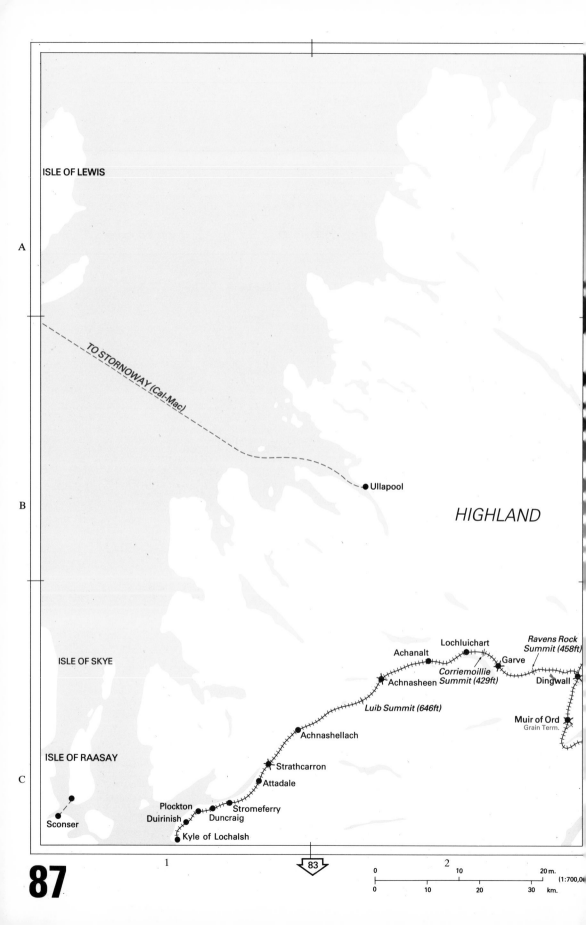

ISLE OF LEWIS

A

TO STORNOWAY (Cal-Mac)

● Ullapool

B

*HIGHLAND*

ISLE OF SKYE

Lochluichart
Achanalt
*Ravens Rock Summit (458ft)*
Garve
*Corriemoillie Summit (429ft)*
Achnasheen
Dingwall

*Luib Summit (646ft)*

Achnashellach

ISLE OF RAASAY

Muir of Ord
Grain Term.

C

Strathcarron
Attadale

Plockton
Stromeferry
Duirinish      Duncraig
Sconser
Kyle of Lochalsh

**87**

1

⟱ 83

2

| 0 | | 10 | | 20 m. |

(1:700,00

| 0 | 10 | 20 | 30 | km. |

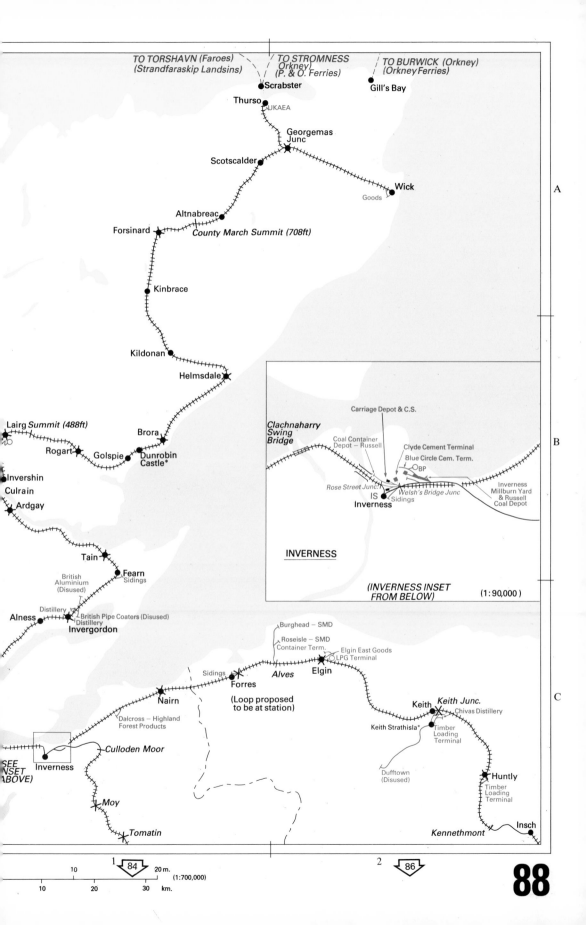

TO TORSHAVN (Faroes)
(Strandfaraskip Landsins)

TO STROMNESS (Orkney)
(P. & O. Ferries)

TO BURWICK (Orkney)
(Orkney Ferries)

● Scrabster

● Gill's Bay

Thurso ●
UKAEA

Georgemas
Junc

Scotscalder ●

● Wick

Goods

A

Altnabreac ●

Forsinard ●        *County March Summit (708ft)*

● Kinbrace

● Kildonan

Helmsdale ●

Lairg *Summit (488ft)*

● Brora

Rogart ●      Golspie ●   Dunrobin
                         Castle*

● Invershin
● Culrain
● Ardgay

*Clachnaharry
Swing
Bridge*

Carriage Depot & C.S.

Coal Container
Depot — Russell

Clyde Cement Terminal

Blue Circle Cem. Term.

○ BP

B

*Rose Street Junc.*          Welsh's Bridge Junc
IS          Sidings
**Inverness**

Inverness
Millburn Yard
& Russell
Coal Depot

Tain ●

British
Aluminium
(Disused)      Sidings
● Fearn

Distillery
● Alness       British Pipe Coaters (Disused)
Distillery
**Invergordon**

**INVERNESS**

**(INVERNESS INSET
FROM BELOW)**          (1 : 90,000 )

Burghead — SMD

Roseisle — SMD
Container Term.      Elgin East Goods
Sidings              LPG Terminal
                     ● Elgin
Forres ●      *Alves*

Nairn ●

(Loop proposed
to be at station)

Keith      *Keith Junc.*
                     Chivas Distillery

C

Dalcross – Highland
Forest Products

Keith Strathisla*    Timber
                     Loading
                     Terminal

● Culloden Moor

*SEE
INSET
ABOVE)*
**Inverness**

Dufftown
(Disused)

● Huntly

Timber
Loading
Terminal

Moy

*Kennethmont*          ● Insch

Tomatin

10        20        30   km.

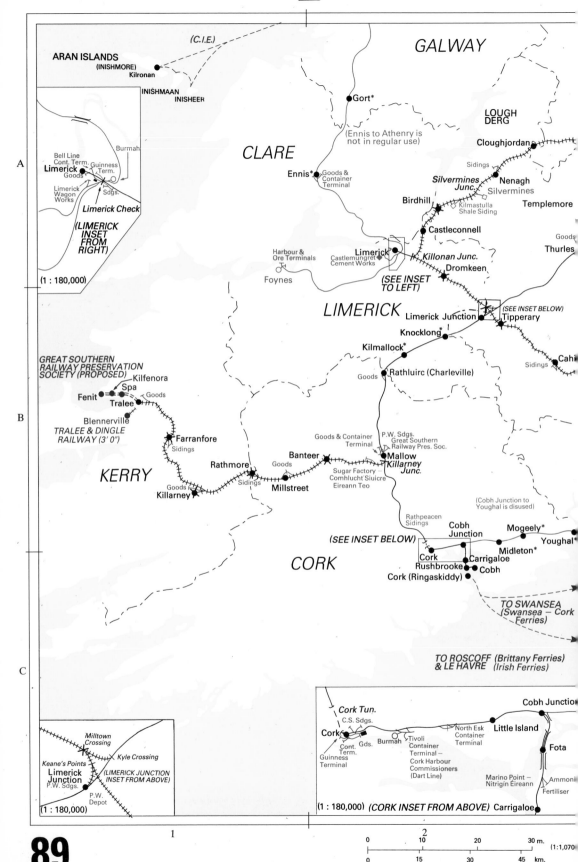

GALWAY

ARAN ISLANDS
(INISHMORE)
Kilronan
(C.I.E.)

INISHMAAN
INISHEER

LOUGH
DERG

Gort*

CLARE

Cloughjordan

Sidings

Silvermines
Junc.

Silvermines

Nenagh

Templemore

Ennis*

Goods &
Container
Terminal

Birdhill

Kilmastulla
Shale Siding

Castleconnell

Thurles

Goods

Bell Line
Cont. Term.
Limerick
Goods

Guinness
Term.

Burmah

Harbour &
Ore Terminals

Castlemungret
Cement Works

Limerick

Killonan Junc.

Dromkeen

Limerick
Wagon
Works

Sdgs.

Foynes

(SEE INSET
TO LEFT)

A

Limerick Check

(LIMERICK
INSET
FROM
RIGHT)

LIMERICK

Limerick Junction

(SEE INSET BELOW)
Tipperary

(1 : 180,000)

Knocklong*

Kilmallock*

Cah

GREAT SOUTHERN
RAILWAY PRESERVATION
SOCIETY (PROPOSED)

Kilfenora

Spa

Fenit

Tralee

Goods

Blennerville

TRALEE & DINGLE
RAILWAY (3' 0")

Farranfore

Sidings

Rathmore

Banteer

B

KERRY

Millstreet

Killarney

Sidings

Goods

Sidings

Goods

Rathluirc (Charleville)

Goods

Sidings

Goods & Container
Terminal

P.W. Sdgs.
Great Southern
Railway Pres. Soc.

Mallow

Killarney
Junc.

Sugar Factory –
Comhlucht Siuicre
Eireann Teo

Rathpeacen
Sidings

Cobh
Junction

(Cobh Junction to
Youghal is disused)

Mogeely*

Youghal

(SEE INSET BELOW)

CORK

Cork

Midleton*

Carrigaloe

Rushbrooke

Cobh

Cork (Ringaskiddy)

TO SWANSEA
(Swansea – Cork
Ferries)

C

TO ROSCOFF (Brittany Ferries)
& LE HAVRE (Irish Ferries)

Milltown
Crossing

Kyle Crossing

Keane's Points

Limerick
Junction

P.W. Sdgs.

(LIMERICK JUNCTION
INSET FROM ABOVE)

P.W.
Depot

(1 : 180,000)

Cork Tun.

C.S. Sdgs.

Cork

Cont.
Term.

Guinness
Terminal

Gds.

Burmah

Tivoli
Container
Terminal –
Cork Harbour
Commissioners
(Dart Line)

North Esk
Container Terminal

Cobh Junctio

Little Island

Fota

Marino Point –
Nitrigin Eireann

Ammoni
Fertiliser

(1 : 180,000) (CORK INSET FROM ABOVE) Carrigaloe

1

2
10

20

30 m.

(1:1,070)

0

15

30

45 km.

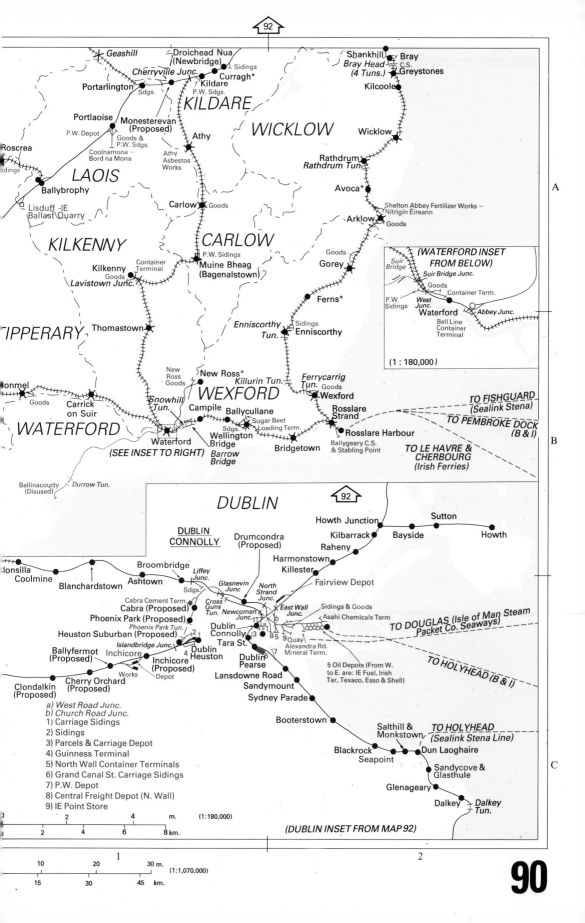

(Belfast Link to Yorkgate
due to open 1992/3, to
Belfast Central 1994/5)

Clipperstown
Downshire
Carrickfergus
BELFAST
LOUGH
Trooperslane
Greenisland
P.W. Siding
TO DOUGLAS (I of M. S.P. Co.)
Jordanstown
DONEGAL
Bleach Green Junc.
Whiteabbey
Helen's
Bay
Carnalea
Seahill
Crawfordsburn
Bangor
Bangor
West
Craigavad *
Ulster
Folk Museum
Cultra
Marino
Holywood
(BELFAST INSET FROM MAP 92)

A

YORK ROAD

Pollock
Dock

N.I.R. Workshops
Belfast
Yorkgate
Belfast
York Road
(Under
construction)
Central
Service
Depot
(To close)
Sydenham
Belfast Great
Victoria St.
(Projected
railway)
Cont. T.
Bridge End
BELFAST CENTRAL
Belfast Central
Belfast City Hospital
Cem.
Botanic
Guinness
Adelaide
P.W.
Depot
Balmoral

0          2 m
|----|----|
0    2    4 km          (1:180,000)

Container
Terminal
Cement
Term.
Sligo Quay –
Deep Water
Irish Tar Co.
Oil
Sligo
LEITRIM

LOWE
LOUG
ERNE

Colloney

MAYO
Container Term.
for Asahi Chems.
Ballina
SLIGO
Ballymote

B

Foxford
Boyle
Carrick- on-Shar
Sidings

D

Sidings
Manulla Junction
ROSCOMMON
Sidings &
Timber Term.
Castlebar
Balla
Westport
Ballyhaunis
Castlerea
P.W. Sdgs.
Claremorris
Goods
Carriage
Stabling
LOUGH
MASK
(Not in regular use)
Roscommon
Sidings
LOUGH
REE
Knockcroghery
LOUGH
CORRIB
West of
Ireland
Steam Rly.
Assoc.
Tuam *
(Not in regular use)
Ballyglunin *
(Castletown)

C

GALWAY
Attymon
Sidings
Ath
Sidings
Athenry
Woodlawn
Ballinasloe
Galway
Goods
Goods
(Not in regular use)

1
89
2

0    10    20    30
|----|----|----|----|
0    15    30    45    km.          (1:1,0

**91**

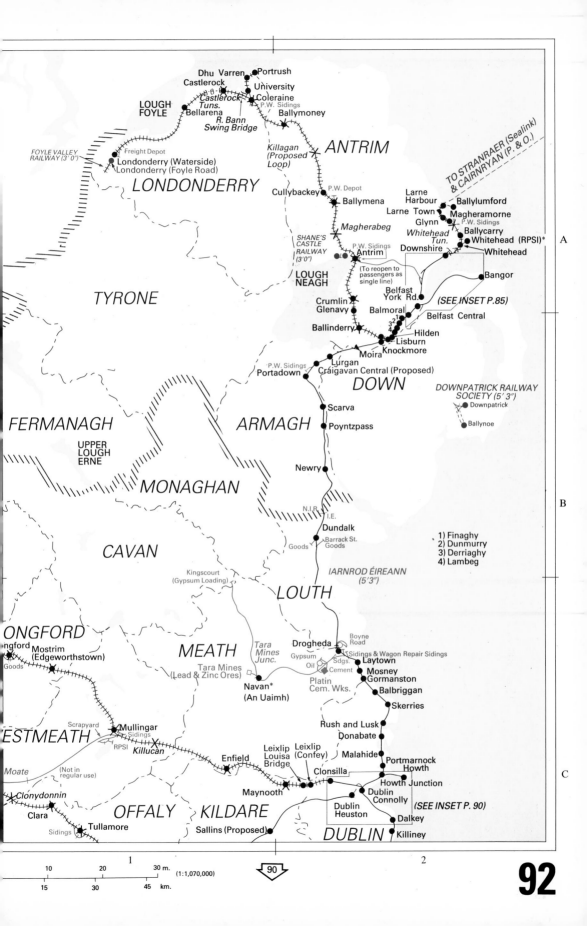

Portrush
Dhu Varren
University
Castlerock
Coleraine
LOUGH FOYLE
Castlerock Tuns.
Bellarena
R. Bann Swing Bridge
P.W. Sidings
Ballymoney

FOYLE VALLEY RAILWAY (3' 0")
Freight Depot
Londonderry (Waterside)
Londonderry (Foyle Road)

LONDONDERRY

Killagan (Proposed Loop)

ANTRIM

TO STRANRAER (Sealink) & CAIRNRYAN (P. & O.)

Cullybackey
P.W. Depot
Ballymena

Larne Harbour
Ballylumford
Larne Town
Magheramorne
Glynn
P.W. Sidings
Whitehead Tun.
Ballycarry
Whitehead (RPSI)*
Whitehead

Magherabeg
Downshire

A

TYRONE

SHANE'S CASTLE RAILWAY (3'0")
P.W. Sidings
Antrim

LOUGH NEAGH

(To reopen to passengers as single line)

Belfast York Rd.
Bangor

(SEE INSET P.85)

Crumlin
Glenavy
Balmoral
Belfast Central

Ballinderry
1
3 2
4
Hilden
Lisburn
Moira
Knockmore

Lurgan
Portadown
P.W. Sidings
Craigavon Central (Proposed)

DOWN

DOWNPATRICK RAILWAY SOCIETY (5' 3")
Downpatrick

Scarva

FERMANAGH

ARMAGH

Poyntzpass

Ballynoe

UPPER LOUGH ERNE

Newry

B

MONAGHAN

N.I.R.
I.E.

CAVAN

Dundalk
Barrack St. Goods
Goods

1) Finaghy
2) Dunmurry
3) Derriaghy
4) Lambeg

Kingscourt (Gypsum Loading)

LOUTH

IARNROD ÉIREANN (5'3")

ONGFORD
ngford
Mostrim (Edgeworthstown)
Goods

MEATH

Tara Mines Junc.
Tara Mines (Lead & Zinc Ores)
Navan* (An Uaimh)

Drogheda
Boyne Road
Sidings & Wagon Repair Sidings
Gypsum
Oil
Cement
Platin Cem. Wks.
Laytown
Mosney
Gormanston
Balbriggan
Skerries

ESTMEATH
Scrapyard
Mullingar
Sidings
RPSI
Killucan

Rush and Lusk
Donabate

Moate
(Not in regular use)

Enfield
Leixlip Louisa Bridge
Leixlip (Confey)
Clonsilla

Malahide
Portmarnock
Howth
Howth Junction

C

Clonydonnin
Clara
Sidings
Tullamore

OFFALY
KILDARE

Maynooth

Dublin Heuston
Dublin Connolly
(SEE INSET P. 90)

Sallins (Proposed)

DUBLIN
Dalkey
Killiney

1
10    20    30 m.
15    30    45 km.
(1:1,070,000)

90

2

**92**

# ELECTRIFICATION MAP

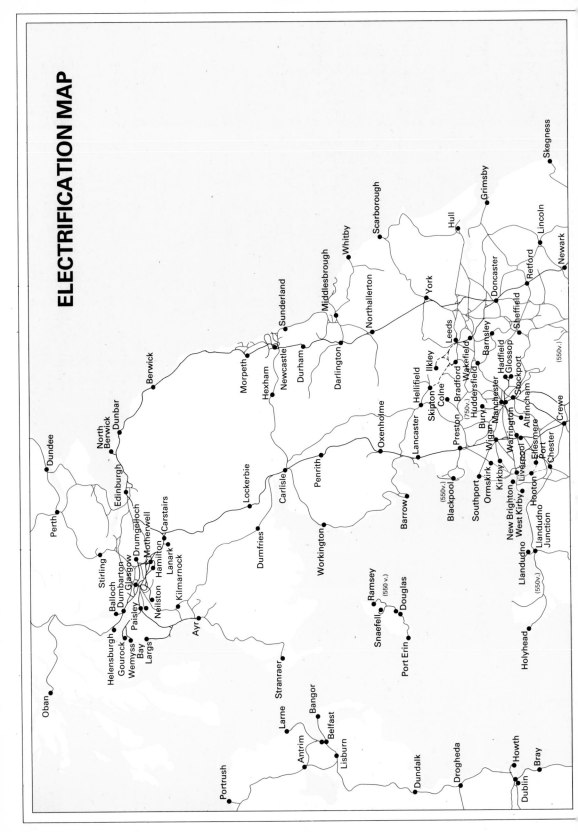

93

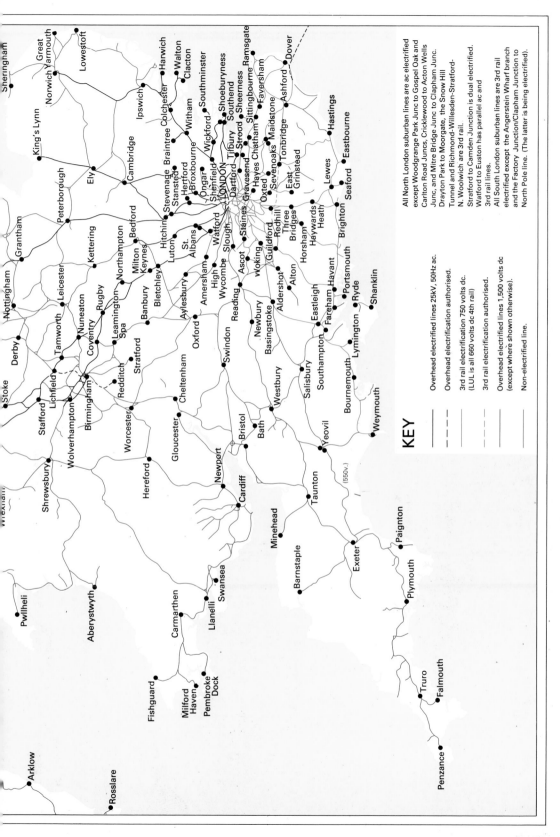

## KEY

Overhead electrified lines 25kV, 50Hz ac.

Overhead electrification authorised.

3rd rail electrification 750 volts dc.
(LUL is all 660 volts dc 4th rail)

3rd rail electrification authorised.

Overhead electrified lines 1,500 volts dc
(except where shown otherwise).

Non-electrified line.

All North London suburban lines are ac electrified except Woodgrange Park Junc to Gospel Oak and Carlton Road Juncs, Cricklewood to Acton Wells Junc, and Mitre Bridge Junc to Clapham Junc. Drayton Park to Moorgate, the Snow Hill Tunnel and Richmond-Willesden-Stratford-N. Woolwich are 3rd rail.
Stratford to Camden Junction is dual electrified. Watford to Euston has parallel ac and 3rd rail lines.
All South London suburban lines are 3rd rail electrified except the Angerstein Wharf branch and the Factory Junction/Clapham Junction to North Pole line. (The latter is being electrified).

# INDEX

All passenger stations are included in this index. Freight terminals, junction names, tunnels and other significant locations are indexed where their names or map references differ from an adjoining passenger station.

101

108

113

114

# INDEX TO BRITISH RAIL
## LOCOMOTIVE STABLING POINTS,
## CARRIAGE DEPOTS & LOCOMOTIVE WORKS